FAITH

In Search of
Greater Glory in Sport

with Gerard Gallagher

HEROBOOKS

PUBLISHED BY HERO BOOKS
1 WOODVILLE GREEN
LUCAN
CO. DUBLIN
IRELAND

Hero Books is an imprint of Umbrella Publishing
First Published 2022

ISBN: 9781910827567

Cover design and formatting: jessica@viitaladesign.com
Photographs: Inpho

dedication

'Whatever you do, do everything
for the glory of God.'
1 Corinthians 10:31

contents

introduction

SPORT HAS THE capacity to bring people together, crossing barriers and bringing unity to spectators and participants. Sport can bring us all moments of joy, despair, hope and heartache.

It has been said that sport does not build character, so much as reveal it, which is why so many of us love feasting our eyes on the sporting arena. Occasionally, we might not care who wins or who loses, but still remain overwhelmed by the courage, resolve, humility and grace that is on view.

Popular culture has been deeply influenced by sport's capacity to engage huge crowds on a global scale. It also can transcend language, geography, social and economic barriers. Sport has been part of human activity for many centuries. Whether it was the individual person using some leisure time, or the competitive first Olympians. From the spectacle of the crowds in the Colosseum in Rome, to our modern stadiums full of cheering fans.

The roar of the crowd is something that can send a chill down the spine of the participant or the spectator. At times, sport can help people escape from life's travails and enter a communion of participation with others. This oneness is something many can relate to. The common experience of sport can bring people together regardless of their differences.

Most people on the planet have experienced attending some type of sporting event. Whether they were in the grandstand or watching on television, sport has the capacity to engage the spectator and help those who are watching to escape and be in communion with others.

Sport changed radically over the last century. It moved from the local community towards the world of commercial influence and other agendas of success and prestige. While sport helps the supporter escape, it can also be a gateway for those practicing to escape poverty, injustice… or just 'life'. Sport can go beyond entertainment. It can become a way of life for some. It has rituals and rhythms that can shape and form a person. Values that can last a lifetime.

FOR SOME OBSERVERS, sport has replaced the religious experience. It has replaced the rituals and communal gatherings of religion with a secular replacement. Our stadiums and pitches have become the new cathedrals and temples.

Sports people have developed and nurtured rituals and traditions to support their personal beliefs. These rituals might be religious or just superstitions. Regardless, these actions can propel the person to do better and achieve higher goals. These acts are like an offering of hope, giving something in the hope of achieving a dream!

Sport can give hope. Sport can help us live a better tomorrow. Sport can bring individuals meaning. It can strengthen a community. Sport has a deserved place in civic society. Sport and religion overlap in that they can teach people values, rules, respect and understanding.

Religion and faith are experienced globally. It is the same with sport. In the crossroads of life, a dialogue between what motivates the sports person and the religious person overlap. Whilst secularism would like religion and faith to separate, many individual practitioners integrate both values in different ways. As our churches shrink in attendance, our stadiums and thirst for participation in sport has increased.

SEVERAL YEARS AGO, I joined a local gym. It was a new experience. Getting fit was no longer just the aim of attending the gym. A shift had taken place. Personal grooming and the concerns for personal health had shifted towards an almost worship of the body and its physical dimension. Body art now was almost the norm.

People now are willing to pay to follow a hard exercise programme, rigorous diets and even drug supplements to enhance their outer appearance. I often wonder what this outer manifestation is trying to replace on the inside. This might be what religious people call the soul!

What is the essence and purpose of all this drive and passion? As our culture becomes emptier of common values, the role of the personal value and individuals leads to this shift towards a search for life balance through being body beautiful and fit.

Instead of sport helping the person grow and develop into their fullest potential, sport can enslave people to cultural fads and fashion concealed under the notion that it helps us be a better, healthier person.

Gone are the days when you could just turn up to play sport in whatever was handy to wear. Sporting culture almost dictates that you must wear a certain type of apparel, look a certain way and fit in. This is part of the economics of sport, because sport is also a business. Sport attracts money. This can also contribute towards the reality of victory at all costs. This can move sport from something that unites, to one that can divide.

There is a generosity of sport too. There still exists the selfless and idealistic amongst us who try to nurture and guide young people on the path towards their chosen sport. This can unveil the positive side of humanity, through sport, and can be a sign of hope, teaching virtue and commitment.

SPORT HAS BEEN conditioned by the culture of the day, and has been able to enculturate values and permeate society. In Ireland, this is true of the Gaelic Athletic Association, similar to other national and international sporting bodies. This goes back to ancient Greece. One of the underlying concepts of the modern Olympics is that sport can assist and recover the notion of being a human community.

The values of the Olympic charter were ecumenical in their tone, affirming all individuals had the right to participate. There is a balance in sport between the formative and educational and personal development of the individual vs the notion of winning a contest or breaking records.

There are historical roots of sport also being balanced, between the need to be a good soldier or warrior vs improving the personal education of the soldier in society.

Modern sport has new challenges, with large corporations influencing the competitive edge of sports stars trying to win at all costs. It could be argued that doping, cheating and dishonesty has always been part of sport. However, in the 20th century this became mainstream with the rise of institutional doping of East German and Russian athletes, as well as individuals in athletics and cycling. There are now few sports which have not been affected by the breakdown in discipline of fair play, and the emergence of systematic cheating. To win at all costs can distract from the fairness of sport.

Sport is a leisure pursuit, an achievement pursuit, a mode of obedience to the drive to self-display, a means for young people to meet, and a means of symbolic cultural exchange. Sport at times has been called a form of a peace movement – in that it can help to heal division and serve as a form of social justice and fairness.

Sport is something that can engage an individual in personal pursuits. It has a social dimension of participating with others in common interests or in teams. It can even involve elites and amateurs taking part alongside each other... think of the New York Marathon and of 80,000 participants all going in the same directions for different reasons.

THE CHURCH HAS had an off-on interest in sport over the centuries. From the writings of St Paul to the Fathers of the Church referencing combat, fatigue and victory as images of the Christian life. The early Christians in the catacombs can be depicted as Christ's athletes. There were many centuries where sport was not referenced. However, in the 20th century almost every pope from Pius XII to Pope Francis, and especially Pope John Paul II, have referred to sport and faith.

For centuries sport was something not really commentated on by the Church. That changed when Pope Pius XII sent a message of support to those attending the Olympics in Melbourne. Whilst reflecting on the writing of St Paul (1 Cor 10:31) he noted, 'How can the Church not be interested in sport?' He also noted that 'the human body... is God's masterpiece.'

The Church was reawakening and reaching out to new cultural movements. It was noticing that one of the signs of the times, sport was an important vehicle towards people fulfilling their potential. This relates to the religious notion of living life to the fullest. All the Popes since have reflected in different ways on the connection of sport and faith, however, this dialogue of faith and the culture of sport is still in its early days.

Pope Saint John Paul II noted frequently how solidarity in sport, 'can encourage young people to develop important values such as loyalty, perseverance, friendship, sharing and solidarity'. Following the Sydney Olympics in 2000, he remarked about how great athletes, sacrificed themselves consistently to achieve results. The logic of sport, he said, especially Olympic sports, 'is also the logic of life: without sacrifices, important results are not obtained, or even genuine satisfaction'.

Pope John Paul II could relate to sport. He was a keen participant in many sports… playing soccer, and skiing, and swimming. His early ministry was shaped by the outdoors. He knew the value of competition and physical challenges, and athletes and sports people could relate to his shared experience of understanding sport.

He was convinced that sport must be considered not just a source of physical well-being but also as an ideal of courageous and life-giving, where individuals and society can fully renew themselves. He also stressed the educational value of sport which can relate the values of love of life, spirit of sacrifice, fair play, perseverance, respect for others, friendship, community and solidarity.

In 2005 the Holy See hosted an international seminar on *'The World of Sport Today: A field of Christian Mission.'* The Church began to see it had a role as an observer of sport and at the service of mission and hope.

Pope Francis has also offered some reflections on sport. He said that sport, 'is a human activity of great value, able to enrich people's lives; it is enjoyed by men and women of every nation, ethnic group and religious belonging'. He explained that the Olympic motto *'altius, citius, fortius'* (Latin for *'Faster, Higher, Stronger'*) is 'an invitation to develop the talents that God has given us'.

Later in these pages, and in their own words, many sportsmen and women will reflect on their motivations, their values, and their key learnings in life. Some will reflect on their faith. Reflecting on life and how sport and faith intersect is a conversation worth having.

There is no such thing as the perfect Christian. Neither is there any such thing as the perfect athlete. Both Christians and sports people strive for perfection.

THERE'S THE DRAMA of sport too. Entire nations can hold their breath as we watch an event! But there is no less drama elicited when an individual, perhaps with very few people in attendance, fulfils a personal dream.

We might idolise some sporting figures and place them on pedestals. But, every single day, 'ordinary people' find something special something within themselves and discover that they can make their ordinary… extraordinary.

Many of us will never achieve the greatness of some of the people who open up about their lives in this book. However, behind every glorious moment, every single achievement, there lies a personal story of a beginning, of graft and dreams, of hard work, and enlightenment.

This is not a book about sport, and sport alone. It is a book that looks at sport through the lens of the spiritual. Some of the people you will meet talk about their own journey in sport and some of the life lessons that they have learned.

A few have fulfilled their dreams. A few have yet to do that.

But each person was open to talk about their sporting life, and their faith, and often the struggles discerning and figuring out their spiritual life. Just like us 'ordinary people' the question of faith, and the meaning of life, remain alive for these brilliant performers.

Many are at different stages of reflecting on their faith and life.

There is a song from ABBA that speaks of '*The winner takes it all.*' However, as you read these conversations you will see that while some of these sporting heroes have fulfilled their dreams and have reached a finish line, others have been happy to have had an honest go at trying to be the best they could possibly be!

Isn't that the Greater Glory?

Gerard Gallagher
August 2022

GAA
fields

'You have to be delicate and respect
people's faith and beliefs, but none of
them challenged me and they all went
along with it! Maybe that's leadership.'

ciarán carey

HURLER

CIARÁN CAREY WAS a swashbuckling hurler, who enthralled not just Limerick supporters, but mostly anyone in the stadium when he was playing. A son of the famed parish of Patrickswell, he was centre-back for his county through the 1990s, helping himself and those alongside him collect two Munster titles and two National League titles. Ciáran was also personally honoured with three All Star awards.

After retiring from playing he became involved in team management and coaching. At club level he has taken charge of the Tournafulla and Granagh-Ballingarry sides in hurling and camogie respectively. He began county coaching career when he was appointed manager of the Limerick senior camogie team in 2007. He subsequently took charge of the Limerick under-21 hurling team, as well as being a selector with the Limerick senior hurling team under Dónal O'Grady. In November 2013, he was appointed for a second spell as manager of the Limerick under-21s. He also returned to education as a mature student to train in counselling.

The Small Village

He grew up in Patrickwell, in a small village, but one of a big family of 10. He notes that hurling was integral to his life.

He lived beside the local pitch. 'It saved a lot of lads' lives, and kept us focused and gave us confidence. As a young lad, I grabbed onto it. I wasn't the greatest at school. Looking back, I didn't apply myself in school... I was the lad at the back keeping a low profile. I was a small boy in primary school but good at hurling, and football and soccer.

'I was good at anything. I grasped onto it at an early age. The more I played, the better I felt and the more I delivered the goods, the better I felt again. Together with my brothers we all played at underage and later we all at some point played in the senior team together. I got the passion for hurling early. I started to play senior at 16... catapulted straight in with the adults! It was a mighty baptism.'

Some of his early memories of faith include preparing for his First Holy Communion. He remembers having the prayer book, the rosary beads, a miraculous medal... and the rehearsal in his local parish church. He comes from a family where attending Mass was important. Going to Mass meant getting dressed up, looking well. However, he admits that like other teenagers he gradually lost the habit and fell into the pattern of only attending church for holy days and weddings, Christmas and Easter.

Ciarán's playing career was part of an amazing era of Limerick hurling. For him, it all began with the influence of his older brothers. Another great inspiration for him was the legendary Cork hurling and football star, Jimmy Barry Murphy. Rahoon-Newcastle.

Ciarán was part of the team that won an All-Ireland Minor Championship when he was aged just 14. He reminisces about that. 'That had a huge effect on me. I had it sussed then that this was what I wanted.

'I wanted to win everything possible. I wanted to get there.'

Regrettably for him, it was a dream that was not going to come true. He did not get to win *everything*. 'In hindsight, I did get there but I didn't get the medal. But sure, does it matter?' For Ciarán the only medal, and ultimate honour, he did not achieve was an All-Ireland senior championship medal... a Celtic Cross. However, he is kind to himself now and is at peace with that, and the fact that it remained an unfulfilled dream.

'I am at peace with all that. You do get asked questions about not getting the All-Ireland. Let's be clear, I was there for 15, 16, 17 years playing at the highest level... for such a long time. Give me that over a short number of years playing and an All-Ireland medal! I would probably pick my long career with club and county and the longevity of it.'

He contrasts the development of the game from his time. 'When you look at systems and modern play, the set-up of my day... it is night and day. In my day we had to figure out many aspects of it ourselves. I did set the bar very high for myself during my career, in every game.

'I brought the fullness of myself to every game. I was driven and kept that mentality. There remains serious bonds of friendship with all the lads I played with. There's the camaraderie... the roar of the crowd... the marching behind the band at a final. So much to be grateful for!

'I put a huge pressure on myself, no matter what jersey I wore, to perform at my highest. If the medals came, they came. Yet there was disappointment too obviously. I am at peace as I look back and very much full of pride at the level of my commitment. Others had a different attitude. I did hope some of my actions would rub off. You see, there was no hiding in the teams that I played with. You had to give everything!'

Pilgrimage of Discovery and Recovery

It wasn't all easy for Ciarán. His life was one lived at a high pace and of constant drama. He notes how his life became affected directly by his addiction to alcohol. He battled this addiction for 20 years. 'It won every battle. I tried everything.'

The happiness he was looking for was not to be discovered there, as he would later experience. He points out he found Jesus by accident. He had nothing else to try or to turn towards. His wife of many years stood by him and it was she who suggested to him, a pilgrimage to Medjugorje. At that point in his life, he says he would have gone to Iraq if he could find inner peace there.

This was his rock bottom, praying that he might not wake up the next morning. For Ciarán, his personal journey over the last 10 years has been his best version of himself, and he continues his path on the road of recovery.

He puts it this way! 'My wife never gave up on me. She was amazing. She saw the true qualities that were in me. My addiction had my character flattened. She came up with the ideas and whatever she would propose, I would say okay. I was a broken person going over to Medjugorje.'

A Point for the Ages

IT WAS CALLED a 'Game for the Ages'... and it ended with a 'Point for the Ages'. Ciaran Carey racing up the length of the field at the very end of a pulsating Munster semi-final against Clare in the Gaelic Grounds in Limerick in 1996. The game would end 1-13 to 0-15, thanks to the Carey score.

Clare looked to have done enough to build a three-point lead as the game closed but then Limerick fired up again – three quick-fire points from Barry Foley (two) and Gary Kirby... before Carey's magical finish.

'The four most agonising seconds of my life,' recalled Clare captain Anthony Daly in a crestfallen Clare dressing-room afterwards. 'The last man you would want to see coming up the field with a ball like that.'

Carey was typically modest. 'I was in a position then to say, "Yeah, okay, we might have a crack here". There was someone on my tail (Fergal Hegarty) all the time. I didn't know who it was. I just dropped the shoulder to the left, jinked to the right, and put it over on the bad side.'

Brian Lohan, Clare's inspirational full-back, saw it all unfold. 'With the heat, if you had said if a fella gets a ball on his own 45 and takes off... if he gets to 25 metres out, he'll be doing awful well to have the strength to hit the ball over the bar, given what had gone in the previous 73 minutes,' says Lohan. 'It was an iconic score, you have to say.'

•••

Whilst on the pilgrimage, he participated fully on the programme... the talks, going to Mass, personal prayer time, going to confession... even letting people pray with him and over him. He really let it all unfold in front of him. He was conscious that something was changing deep inside of him.

In his own words, 'On this journey, I was changing on my journey there. The only way I can explain it, looking back, is that it was Jesus and his mother Mary comforting and helping me. I had some beautiful experiences such as 'smelling roses' every night I was there... I got this scent. Other people there told me this was 'Our Lady, healing and helping you'.

Reawakening and Refocusing

Since that initial reawakening of his faith, he has returned again to Medjugorje, to give thanks. He now knows his faith is not something to be kept private or hidden. To have faith, he knows he needs to give it away.

'This was my first adult relationship with Jesus/God. It was when I needed help with my hands up in the air that God helped. Men are full of ego. We are *full* of ego, and you can't be seen to be soft. This is a hard environment for men. Now, thankfully, I have the courage to put my hands up and not be afraid to tell people... I am a believer.'

Throughout his career Ciarán had some simple and private ways of bringing his faith into his personal preparations. No one knew he was doing anything. Yet, in amusement he notes the modern player in soccer coming out and making a show of themselves blessing themselves or touching the pitch. Yes, in his day, he did pray privately before a match.

'I got into the habit of 30 minutes before the match, whether it was playing for club, county or soccer, I would slip away up to the shower or the toilet. I would take a smoke and have a chat with the Lord. I would pray and just have a chat to Jesus. He really knows what is in your heart. It was never selfish.

'My prayer was just a word to give my best, to have the legs to keep running... get no injury. It was never to be Man of the Match or win a medal... funny enough.'

He kept these little rituals alive throughout his career. He now observes that God was listening to his prayer and looked after him. His private prayer was an important part of his preparation.

He has no recollection, in all his years, of a manager leading a prayer in the dressing-room. And, in his own management methods, he was aware not every player was into prayer, faith or holy matter. After his experiences in Medjugorje many of his colleagues would be aware of his faith. He waited until a county final before introducing it to the dressing-room! 'I timed it for the county final. I invited the local priest up to say a prayer. Fr Eamon came in to bless us and he said a prayer. In true Irish style, we left it at that.'

He also recalls another episode when he was managing the Kerry hurling team in 2005. 'We were playing a championship match against Offaly in Tullamore. I was rooming with Mark and we were going over a few last minute things. We were chatting and I was tossing in the bed. I said to him, I think we are forgetting something for tomorrow. I didn't know what box I had not ticked. Then, like a bolt of lightning, I realised we had no Mass planned for the morning. So, picture this... I phoned Fr Chris O'Donnell back in Limerick around midnight and explained the scenario. The conversation veered towards me asking him did he know a priest up around Portlaoise or Kildare to say a Mass.

'He told me to leave it with him. Later he texted back to say he would be up at 8am to say Mass in the morning. This was not on the schedule. I was up first in the morning to meet the lads at breakfast. I met them, told them there was change in the plan and that there would be Mass at 8. I gave them no choice... they all had to go!

'Even more ironic, they were all in for Mass! You have to be delicate and respect people's faith and beliefs, but none of them challenged me and they all went along with it! Maybe that's leadership.'

New Ways

Ciarán now works as a counsellor in Limerick. He is very much aware of people's alternative values, beliefs... and maybe no faith tradition. He has seen and experienced many different realities and is empathetic and aware that in some people's lives, that might be broken. While respecting boundaries, if faith matters emerge, he is very happy to include that as part of the overall process.

He firmly believes God supports him in all that he does in life, including his work. The fighter on the hurling field is still very much able to get into the trenches to talk about God and life with those who have lost their way. His talents are now directed in new ways. He takes inspiration from people who have lived life through challenging circumstances, noting Pope John Paul II, Muhammad Ali and Nelson Mandela. Ultimately though, his wife is the influence that helped him to find a new path in life after sport.

Ciarán is a man still on a mission and grateful for his faith. When talking about what he'd like to be remembered for, with a glint in his eye he says with the conviction of the hurler scoring the winning point, 'A humble and simple hurler… others will write it, my wife will take care of that!'

●●●

'I come from a traditional Catholic family. Good Irish identity too. Growing up it was normal to go to Mass as a family. There was a good bit of religion in both primary and secondary school. Faith was all around me.'

rena buckley

CAMOGIE PLAYER AND GAELIC FOOTBALLER

THROUGHOUT HER CAREER, Rena Buckley was unstoppable. Unbeatable. She finished up her career as a camogie and gaelic football legend, and one of Irish most decorated GAA players of all time. Between 2005 and '17 Rena won 18 All-Ireland Senior Championships. All in the majestic red of Cork. She has also represented Munster and Ireland.

Rena was also a true leader on the field. In 2012 she captained Cork when they won the All-Ireland Ladies Football Championship and, in 2017, she captained Cork when they won the All-Ireland Camogie Championship. She was the first player to captain Cork to both All-Ireland championships. She was also named as an All Star on 11 occasions. It's no wonder, she has a place of honour, despite her young age, in the GAA Museum.

She was named joint winner of the *The Irish Times* Sportswoman of the Year in 2015 with her teammate Briege Corkery. That year, Rena and Briege both broke the record for most individual All-Ireland medals, overtaking the 15 won by the Dublin camogie player Kathleen Mills. Rena also represented UCD between 2005 and '09, where she also played camogie and ladies football. She featured in four successive Ashbourne Cup finals, finishing on winning teams in 2007 and '08, and represented the college in the O'Connor Cup winning team in 2006.

She retired from the Cork senior ladies football team after the All-Ireland final in 2016 and finished with the Cork senior camogie team the following season.

The Parish of Inniscarra

Rena is from a small village in Cork called Berrings in the parish of Inniscarra. She was baptised Catherine Susan, but all her life she has been called Rena, just like her grandmother. Inniscarra is an area steeped in the traditions and culture of the gaelic games. Rena notes that neither of her parents, who are not from Inniscarra, had a big relationship with the GAA. That would change with Rena.

'My dad would have had an interest in the gaelic games; he played a little when he was at school. Mum had little interest. She was amongst a generation of women who didn't really play sport, compared to my generation. However, both of my parents had a huge interest in Irish culture. My mother was an Irish and maths teacher. She speaks glorious Irish... I'd say better than formal English!'

Life at home was one of balancing education, familiarity with Irish culture, and going to Mass. For Rena, this was just normal.

'Dad has a huge interest in Irish, Irish culture and nowadays the GAA, so that is how it all fell into place. We didn't speak a lot of Irish growing up. There were moments when we did speak Irish at home, but we speak a little more now, especially since my daughter came along.'

Becoming Rena

'I went to Berrings National School. My older brother was into hurling. He developed a huge grá for hurling and football in school, and we used to play all kinds of games at home. We were always pucking or kicking a ball in some fashion. We progressed from there to joining the local club.'

Soon, Rena would go on to play with many of the local underage teams.

'I joined Donoughmore ladies football club, as Inniscarra did not have a ladies football team. When I was in fourth class in Berrings, the principal started a ladies football team. There was always a camogie team in Berrings for as long as I can remember. We played in the Sciath na Scoil competition, which is a huge primary schools competition in Cork. We reached the final and played against Firmount, which is a school in Donoughmore. A few weeks after that game, Dan O'Mahony from Donoughmore called to the house and asked if I would play football with them. I was absolutely delighted! I then had both a football and camogie club to play with… and I absolutely loved every facet of it.'

Like other young people playing gaelic games, Rena took part in other sports too.

'I was also involved in a lot of athletics as a child. I was a decent runner. However, I leaned towards team sports because I felt there was better fun there.

'Sonia O Sullivan was a huge role model for me when I was growing up. I didn't know her. But she was a Cork girl, internationally known… was world class and I thought she was awesome. Catriona McKernan was also inspirational for me, as she was a runner who had played camogie. I could relate to her! We know that having role models is important for young people playing sport. We all need to have someone to aspire to, and I was very lucky that I certainly had sporting role models to look up to.'

Teenage Kicks

Rena quickly became a dual player of note, playing ladies football for Donoughmore and camogie for Inniscarra.

'There is a strong tradition of camogie in Inniscarra and football in Donoughmore, so while the parishes are next door, there's no big rivalry between the clubs. We had local role models too. Irene O'Keefe from Inniscarra was a Cork camogie player and I went with club mates to support Irene and her colleagues at Croke Park in All-Ireland finals. I wanted to be like her when I was older… just like everyone else.'

Women involved in team sports was natural and nurtured in Cork, at this time.

'Because of where I am from, there is a tradition of women playing, unlike other parts of the country.' Rena continued to excel in sport while she attended secondary school. Whilst still a young teenager, she was selected for her clubs' senior teams.

'I got drafted in with the Donoughmore senior team when I was 14. That year we went on to win the Cork championship and, for the first time in the club's history, the Munster and All-Ireland Championships. That experience gave me huge exposure to very well prepared teams, and talented players and great coaches at a very young age. It was an amazing experience.'

The thirst for winning was with Rena.

'I believe the desire to win is innate. However, being part of that very positive

Equality in Sport

RENA IS ONE of the most decorated GAA players of all time. She has won 18 All-Ireland medals, an unbelievable number! But even after all that, as she told the SportsJoe website, she discovered there was more work to be done in allowing everyone to understand that women in sport are equally as gifted and deserving as men.

She was invited to a club in Cork to present medals. Their under-14 girls and under-12 boys had won championships, but...

'I went along and when I got down there on the night, the lad who invited me took me aside and said, "Look we're really sorry but the GAA team actually don't want you to present the boys with the medals".

'They got some local guy to do it. He was absolutely mortified. He could hardly look at me, he was really embarrassed.

'That's just the mindset of whoever was organising that... we're looking for a shift in that. It's a rare thing but that was 2017... it wasn't 1986.'

•••

sporting culture was excellent in terms of my development as a person and as an athlete. The people involved were very good people, they were serious about everything they did. The set-up was very professional, yet we had great fun and got huge enjoyment from football. That had a big influence on me, especially as a young person.'

Identity and Faith

'I come from a traditional Catholic family. Good Irish identity too. Growing up it was normal to go to Mass as a family. There was a good bit of religion in both primary and secondary school. There was the sacraments, prayers, class Masses and so on. Faith was all around me. In home we regularly said the rosary.'

She does point out that it was not all serious religion. 'Often on long journeys in the car, the rosary was said to keep us quiet!' For Rena, being Catholic and expressing her faith was normal and natural in her home life. As she looks back she recalls how normal this was.

'I have memories of my mum being sick and our local priest visited the house. This was a big event for us. I also have great memories of my grandaunts who were nuns. When they visited it was a big deal.'

Just like other clubs, there was no explicit faith ethos in the dressing-room. Yet it was normal at certain key moments that the club and the local parish would keep connected. 'If we won something, there was usually a function. Our local priest would attend these functions. I also remember when I playing on underage teams with the Cork footballers... under-14, under-16 and minors, one of our selectors was Fr Liam Kelleher. He would regularly say Mass after matches. He would keep us connected with little prayer items and rituals.'

Being Grateful

'I have been very lucky. Much of my success in sport was because I was born at a particular time and place, and surrounded by certain people. I think I remained grounded due to the family, personnel in the clubs and my friends. However, I do understand I generally tend to work hard and I don't rest on my laurels. I am still competitive.

'It is hard to let that competitive instinct go. I love all the aspects of the game. I love all the running, as well the tactical aspect of the games. I have played football, camogie and competed at athletics, as they were the sports which were available to me growing up. I was very lucky in that those sports suited me and my personality. I am grateful for all that.'

Rena goes on to reflect a little deeper on her talent for sport.

'I have been blessed with athleticism. God has given me a talent. However, this blessing needs a work ethic.' God's gifts also need to be reciprocated with hard work.

It was not all plane sailing for Rena, either. Just like other people in sport there were times when she had doubts.

'In my 20s there was a patch where I just wasn't playing well. I spent the winter contemplating what I would do, whether to give up or not? My approach was to get extremely fit. I took up boxing. This contributed to a sort of revival in my career. This gave me a new sense of resilience because I was now in peak condition.'

Just like other people involved in high levels of sport, Rena also had to adapt as she got older. 'I was fast at 18, and slower at 28. I had to adjust my game to suit my body. I wanted to enjoy the last years of my playing career.' Behind all these adjustments Rena had an anxiety.

'My mother had a mild form of MS at this time. I did get worried and anxious that this was a condition I might also develop and that this was affecting me.'

During these years she does note that she was thinking deeply about her life. 'I certainly did reflect deeply. When I attend Mass, that is when I take time to reflect and think about things that are going on for me. I might not have formally prayed, but I certainly was close to it.'

Looking Back and Looking Forward

Rena is now a member of the Irish Society of Chartered Physiotherapists. She was attracted to physiotherapy whilst still at school. 'In school I loved sport. I liked science topics. I was attracted to physio. It is a very non-invasive form of medicine and aids naturally, which contributes to why I love it. I am currently training to be a health coach and I am learning about the different facets of health, including the spiritual. This is really a new area for me. I am now looking at health more holistically and how the spiritual is part of that completeness.

'Over the last couple of years my studies have forced me to think more deeply about my faith and spirituality. Also, during the Covid-19 restrictions many of my connections to faith were stopped. I was a regular Mass-goer… then all that was stopped. It is a journey, and I am still mulling and making my way through these questions. I don't think that ever stops.

'I hear the word sacrifice a lot in dressing-rooms. It is a choice to do something you love, and not a sacrifice. I have missed out socially with friends, weddings… socialising. You can't participate in the drinking culture if you want to get to the top in the world of sport. However, I have no regrets in my choices. I really enjoyed doing what I did. What we did together as a team was a type of spiritual communion and connection.'

She still looks forward to getting into the dressing-room.

'I love the preparation and pre-match rituals. I don't do anything in particular myself because if you forget or can't do it for some reason, that can throw you.' Rena still has future sports targets. 'I would love to run a marathon or maybe a sprint triathlon. I also want to get involved in coaching.'

Soon after the birth of her daughter, she was looking forward to going back training. She still wants to stay connected to sport in her locality.

'I have been blessed all my life. I am really grateful. I have had so much joy through sport. My family and husband have been so supportive in all that I have done. I hope people would remember me as a person who did her best and always had a smile on her face!'

'I lean towards God, who gives sense
and purpose to what my world should
be. Maybe it's not worked out like other
people's understanding. God wants us to
be good and create goodness. For me, that
is trying to be the best that you can be.'

brian mullins

GAELIC FOOTBALLER

BRIAN MULLINS IS one of the truly legendary figures in the GAA. Through the 1970s and 80s he was an inspirational midfielder on the Dublin team which went toe-to-toe with Mick O'Dwyer's legendary Kerry.

Mullins was also a rock for St Vincent's during his playing career, and after hanging up his boots he managed his native county, in addition to Derry. A former school principal, Mullins is now Director of Health Promotion and Sport in UCD.

'I am an Irishman, and I say that because the influences on me range from West Kerry on my mother's side, and West Clare my father's side, and I lived in New York and was part of the Irish Community there. I have also lived in Carndonagh, in Donegal. As a result, I believe that the whole island has had an influence on my character, as well as living and working in urban Dublin in the northside of the city.'

Growing up in Clontarf, Brian was aware of his GAA heritage going back to his uncle Bill Casey, who played for Kerry in the 1930s and 40s. As a young boy in urban Dublin he was always very much aware of his rural roots.

After completing four years of college in Limerick, Brian subsequently returned to Dublin where he first secured a teaching job in Greendale Community School in Kilbarrack.

In 1980 he took 18 months leave of absence from Greendale to complete a Master of Arts in Athletic Administration at New York University. When he returned from the United States, he resumed his teaching post at Greendale and stayed there until 1991. That year he was appointed Head Teacher of Carndonagh Community School in Inishowen. Brian again returned to Dublin in 2000 to take up the role as UCD Director of Sport and, in 2015, the additional role of Director of Health Promotion.

The Early Years

He came from a family with a strong faith, where religion was important. The whole family attended the local parish for Mass. He attended Marlborough School in Dublin 1 and Coláiste Mhuire in Parnell Square, before later attending Thomond College in Limerick, where he completed a Bachelor of Arts in Physical Education and Irish Studies.

One of his earliest memories of faith in the home was the daily praying of the Rosary as a family. In his youth it was common for Irish families to have a family rosary. However, with his brothers, as the spring days grew longer, they tried to get this moment of prayer over early. 'My brothers and I around this time of year often tried to get the rosary on earlier, so that in the brightening days we could get outside… because if we didn't, the whole night was ruined!'

Looking back at his early influences, he explains, 'The spirit of faith is around what you shape in your head about your faith and values. Not everyone does this. It must be a choice for people to reflect on their values, and how that shapes them. Being good is about being God… being the best you can be, and being thoughtful and committed to helping other people. It is about helping those maybe not as fortunate, and maybe not as lucky as you are.'

Initially, he did not intend to be a teacher, but 'drifted' towards PE and working in a school. 'I found that I liked working with and helping younger people grow and get to understand what life was about, and it is a privilege to accompany them as they improve and better themselves as they go along through life. This helped me continually grow also!'

He went on to spend 22 years in a school environment, noting, 'I was in my right place'.

Absorbed in Sport

Brian was always involved in sport during his childhood. He played everything…
cricket, hurling, gaelic football, soccer, cycling. He says, 'We all were sports mad on
the promenade on the Clontarf Road. The passion and the best moments were here.
I learned how to read the ball on the bounce. It was a great grounding in the basics
of sport.' He spent some of his summers in Kerry with his mother's family on his
Uncle Billy's farm. He discovered that his country cousins had fewer boundaries,
and Brian and his brothers decided they were not going to let the Kerry cousins
get the upper-hand. This was almost a premonition of the many great battles on
the field he would have with Kerry's best footballers. 'My brothers and I decided
we were not going to lose! This would remain with me later in life… a life lesson.
When you get onto the pitch, it's every man for himself. It is all or nothing, and
about completely giving of your best.'

Because of his height, he found sport to be easy and natural. He also states
that he was 'blessed with a strong heart'. Being able to 'go the distance' was a
characteristic that he would bring to sport and life at a higher level,

'I can dig deep… I'm resilient. It's all natural, but I had to appreciate it in my
mind and leverage from it.'

He started playing with Dublin in 1974, on the magnificent team being
created by the brilliant Kevin Heffernan. Quickly, he learned that when you lose
big matches, or you lose out to better opponents on any given day, it is through
reflection that you learn and grow. Brian explains that Kevin Heffernan, or Heffo
to the Dublin fans, encouraged a great degree of self-reflection, wanting his
players to think about and reflect on what happened on the field, especially when
things didn't go according to plan.

Heffernan was a master of constructive analysis and leading a reflective
dialogue on learning lessons from defeat. From his own playing days through
the 1950s and 60s with the Dubs, Heffernan was steeped in the tradition of the
county. He would lead Dublin to three All-Irelands, in 1974, '76 and '77. Brian
reflects on some of the wisdom that Kevin used to impart to his players.

'He used to ask, "If you did it again, what would you do differently? Now
you know what you know…." This was long before the modern analysis in the
current game.'

In the Genes

OVER THE COURSE of his career, Brian Mullins won four All-Ireland titles, nine Leinster titles, two National Leagues and two All Star awards, and became a hero of Hill 16 for his inspirational displays in the middle of the field. But, where did it all come from? And was it something in the Mullins' genes? In 2016, Brian chatted with John Harrington on GAA.ie about the question of ancestry, and what special qualities might fall down from the family tree. Because the Dublin colossus is actually a nephew of the great Bill Casey from Lispole, who won four All-Ireland titles with Kerry.

'A grand-uncle of mine, an uncle of Bill Casey, won two All-Irelands with Dublin in 1906 and 1908. He had come up from Kerry. My mother would have suggested that physique-wise I was like him. I have five brothers and none of them are tall. Physique-wise they were more like my father's side of the family.

'When we got into our teens and there was a row between myself and the brothers, they used to tell my mother she brought the wrong baby home because I was so much taller than the rest of them.

'I'm wondering how deep you're going to get into this GAA gene thing, because it's a bit of a minefield. In some respects it's a fascinating idea that the athletic gene or the capacity to play the national games, whether it's hurling or football, are somehow influenced by your ancestry.

'I'm sure across the spectrum of genealogy there's all kinds of associations you can make with people who are successful in business, people who are successful in the profession of law or medicine or whatever. It's the same context about what's handed down from one generation to another.

'Or the famous Irish saying, 'He didn't lick it off the street!'. And the saying as Gaeilge, 'Briseann and dúchas trí shúile an chait'.

•••

The Crash

Brian tells a story about a night he was out with some friends. They were socialising; he wasn't drinking, but was driving. These were the days when people were not required to wear seat belts. His car crashed into a lamp-post. The post entered the car but, miraculously, because Brian was not wearing a seat belt, he had ended up in the back seat due to the impact.

'I think I am a lucky person... very lucky. Because of all the things that have happened to and for me. On that occasion, I ended up in hospital for months. Eventually, all my injuries healed. However, in the moment between losing control of the car and hitting the lamp-post I made my peace, as I thought I was gone. I prepared myself to say hello to whoever and where I was going.'

This near-death experience has had a huge impact on him. In letting go, he believes he was given a new beginning. 'I was surprised as I woke up with bones sticking out of my leg.' His second chance meant a new way of looking at life.

'It was a key moment for me. It wasn't my time, I knew I had another chance, I just had to improve myself! This relates to my spiritual side... my second chance. I had no control... I was out of control for those five seconds. The car was all over the place. There was no control over anything. It was beyond me.

'I gave myself up to whatever happened.'

He is not sure if he was letting go to let God take over. However, his instinct was 'some kind of prayer. I gave thanks instinctively, and said something to my wife... asking her to look after our children.' He mulls over the significance of that moment. 'Was it a prayer... of sorts... maybe?'

For Brian, God has a place in his life. 'I lean towards God, who gives sense and purpose to what my world should be. Maybe it's not worked out like other people's understanding. God wants us to be good and create goodness. For me, that is trying to be the best that you can be.'

He then explains that after the accident he went to New York in 1980 to start post graduate studies.

'It was a new mission in life, an opportunity to do better in my life. I didn't necessarily think of the divine but refocused on my personal vocation to be a better person.'

On Reflection

In the dressing-room with most football teams he played on, he did not witness too many players in moments of prayer or contemplation. This is a common experience where expressions of prayer and faith are very much private to the individual. He does note that when he managed Derry, many of the players expected and enjoyed local priests coming in to pray and even to say Mass. However, he concedes this is most likely due to the cultural nuances of Catholicism in Derry in the last years of the Troubles in Northern Ireland.

'Mass on the Sunday was on the schedule, and I maintained it. It was important for the lads; I could see that it was important to them. For them, checking in with Mass and their Lord was important. Also, they were in the middle of the Troubles. Northern Catholics were different in how they related to their faith.

'It was an identity and a badge that was important for them. It seemed to me that it grounded them more than the lads elsewhere in the country. It wasn't that they were less religious, it was just they had less of a faith identity. But this was a major part of being a young Catholic in the north. The Northern GAA lads had a somewhat different experience than lads playing football anywhere else in the country.'

Kevin Heffernan was a huge figure in his life, and something more than a team manager. He takes personal inspiration from 'working' with Heffernan and observing how he was so gifted in getting the best out of his players. Brian himself was inspired by Nelson Mandela and Che Guevara to bring change. Personally, he remembers Sr Una Collins, a Holy Faith Sister, who inspired people by her faith and a holistic model of school education, teaching people to be good, and leading and living a good life.

Brian believes that everything he was given in life was an opportunity, not a sacrifice. He understood the importance of taking his football career – even if he was an amateur sportsman – seriously, and looking after himself, and never forgetting how fortunate he was to do what he was doing. Another great Dublin coach and mentor, Mickey Whelan stressed this to Mullins.

Brian says that through sport there is an opportunity to instil a code of beliefs... family, tradition and community. Young people, he believes, are always searching for meaning in life. He is impressed by some younger sportspeople who are comfortable speaking about their faith.

All in this Together

Brian Mullins was very much aware that he could not be that 'hungry player and manager' for ever. Like Clint Eastwood, he is now trying to not, 'Let the old man in!' He passionately believes that sport taught him how to depend on every person on his team. This 'we are all in this together' attitude for him is a definition of faith and Church.

Brian is happy with his life and the luck that has come his way, one day at a time. His brother's recent death has also caused him to reflect on the bigger questions in life. To sum up his life, his epitaph would be, 'I tried my best... or tried the best I could!'

●●●

'I would pray for guidance as a
manager, not for victory, because God
is on both sides. We have to use our
talents. If our best is not good enough,
this doesn't mean we are failures!'

seán boylan

GAELIC FOOTBALL MANAGER AND HURLER

SEÁN BOYLAN IS a living legend in the GAA, and he is, of course, synonymous with Meath. Family is important to him. He's an only son with five sisters. His dad was 28 years older than his mother. He tells the story of his dad meeting his mother. They got engaged on the day they met, and were married a month later. No fuss. It was 1939, and his dad wanted to get married as the Second World War was just about to begin. Just after their marriage, his dad wanted to make a trip to Lourdes and Rome. Rome was important to him, as the Vatican was the first State to recognise the Irish Free State. His dad was born in 1880 and was a prominent republican in his earlier years. Seán's father was Brigadier General Seán Boylan. He was a prominent member of the Irish republican movement in the early years of the 20th century, a comrade of many of the signatories of the 1916 Declaration of Independence, and a member of the IRA Army Council.

Seán Boylan Snr had strong principles and a strong faith. He wouldn't take the pledge even though in his life he did not take a drink. Seán Snr was publicly denounced for his role in the Troubles in Ireland by members of the Church, but he still attended Mass at this time. This resolute character was something that young Seán would also echo in his own life. Being his own man.

'I have a very simple faith,' Seán insists, 'based on the fact that God loves us and asks us to return to love him and love our neighbour.'

He recalls some of his early memories of prayer at home. 'The rosary was said every night when I was growing up. Whoever was in the house, they joined in with the rosary too. Like every house, there were some funny moments when we all knelt down to pray, but the rosary was the prayer that my parents said. The philosophy was loving your neighbour and yourself.'

Seán attended the Jesuit college, Belvedere College in Dublin and remembers making his Confirmation in the Pro-Cathedral in 1953, at the age of 10. He was confirmed by Archbishop John Charles McQuaid who was friendly with his dad.

'Going to Belvedere was a big experience,' he points out. 'My sisters and I took the bus in daily to Eccles Street in Dublin to school. You went to class, and you played rugby and hurling. Any homework I had was done on the bus. When I got home, I would have jobs to do. I believe still that if you want to teach me, do it in school, during school hours. When you are home... there's no need for homework!'

For Seán, growing up in Dunboyne was perfect. 'It was a life full of gaelic games, religion, politics, farming, herbs... people and employment,' he explains. 'I thought there was no place like it and I suppose, in truth, there wasn't.'

A Personal Faith

'Our lives were dominated by religion, its practice and the observance of rituals. I was an altar boy too. Our lives seemed to revolve around churches. Every November we would do rounds of the city churches... St Peter's in Phibsboro, Gardiner Street, Clarendon Street, Arran Quay... as well as Whitefriar Street and Church Street. I think this is how I got to know Dublin so well.'

From an early age Sean seriously contemplated becoming a priest. He was attracted towards the Cistercian Order. 'I was not very pious, but I felt I needed God in my life. Whatever talents I had were God-given.'

He has remained connected to God. From the age of 10, he believed his calling in life was to be a Cistercian monk. As a young boy, he was inspired by the writings of the Cistercian Trappist Thomas Merton.

'When I was 10, I was in the Cistercian monastery in Roscrea for a visit,' he continues. 'I happened to stay in the monastery. I absolutely loved the rituals and lifestyle of these monks. I read and still love Thomas Merton and his book

Seven Story Mountain. This was a deeply religious man, and his spiritual life and work life were one. Merton loved a party and enjoying life. I like that. Sometimes in religion people fall in love with the doctrine rather the rule of love. I loved the humanity of Merton. From the age of 10 to 37... all I wanted was to be a Cistercian monk.

'I also wanted to do several other things... work at home, and work with our herbs. I can recall meeting one of the monks, who just said to me, "If you pray for me, I'll pray for you". I remember getting a sense during Matins (prayer) that a voice told me I need God in the world. That challenge never left me. I have always been thankful for God... and to God. I am also close to Laurence Freeman, who would be my spiritual director, a disciple of John Main.'

Seán's discernment took years. After years of social life and agonising about which path to take, the words of his uncle, a priest Willie Quinn resonated. 'Even though it is a great honour and privilege to be a priest, sometimes you can do better work in the world.'

Seán knew that he could do God's work in his daily life.

The Glory of Sport

Meath won the county's first All-Ireland senior football title in 1949. 'Everyone in our club in Dunboyne played hurling. We were hurling mad! We played football too. There were no underage games around this time in Ireland. Meath won the All-Ireland again then, in 1954... we all went mental! Just as other people might have played music, we played hurling and football!'

The ethic of working hard was matched by playing and enjoying his hurling and football. 'We played on the village green as teenagers. You played against older lads, and you learned how to survive!'

In 1961, he recalls, 'I played minor and senior hurling from the age of 17. What I learned from playing, and especially in defeat, was that you can improve... you can go out tomorrow and be better.

'I was fortunate to play hurling for almost 20 years, for Dunboyne and Meath, and we were lucky enough to win a few Division 2 National League titles. I played football too with the club and got picked a few times for the county team also. But if there was a clash between two matches at the time... I would play hurling!'

Managing Meath

'I often wondered what I would do when I finished playing hurling and football. This was 1982. I then got a call from the county chairman, Brian Smyth with the offer to consider managing the county team.' Seán thought it was the job of managing the Meath hurling team that was on the table; in fact, it was the county football team. He considered the offer, and talked to a few people and discovered that there was nobody else who wanted to manage the Meath football team. At this stage, football in the county was at a low ebb.

He points out that there is no magic formula in managing a team. 'It is largely a matter of being in the right place at the right time, and creating the right environment for success.' Over the years, his esoteric training methods would be questioned. But they worked.

'I decided to take on the role for three months, until someone else could be found. This actually was expanded to 23 years as manager! It was extraordinary to see how the whole thing grew, and how we grew as individuals.

'In 1986, we moved our training base to Dalgan Park, outside Navan, the home of the Columbans, a missionary order with connections to Asia and South America. Because we were there, I would tell the lads before a match that there was Mass. I would invite them to go and then say we would have food afterwards... and a team chat. Several players questioned if they had to go. I would tell them, it's your own decision and suit yourself. Other players told me they appreciated being able to attend the Mass as part of the training!'

The rhythm of playing sport in the grounds of Dalgan Park made it very convenient for players to train, and even pray to play harder! The prayer and spiritual side was natural and not forced. 'Our relationship with the Columban Fathers was extraordinary. Some of the missionaries had returned from China or Korea. Some had been prisoners in China. There was Fr Peter Quinn, who was a missionary priest who had played in an All-Ireland final with Mayo in 1951. If he was around, he would attend our training sessions and he'd chat to some of the players. I've met some outstanding priests who were brilliant players of the game.

'We could be training on a Saturday evening... and around 6pm the bell would go. We would all stop and say the Angelus... and then continue. It wasn't asking God for anything, just taking a moment to express our thanks for being able to play.

'We were lucky with the squad of players that we assembled. They were a real band of brothers. These lads gave everything and allowed that little space for the holy to be part of their regime.

'I think, looking back, there were very few players who did not bless themselves before a big match.' These were silent personal prayers.

'I would pray for guidance as a manager, not for victory, because God is on both sides. We have to use our talents. If our best is not good enough, this doesn't mean we are failures!'

There were no coaching badges or courses for trainers in Seán's time as Meath manager. 'I went in as a coach and trainer. There was no title like "manager" back at that time. At that stage I knew more about what I didn't know! I held firm the belief that preparation was crucial. I was very clear in having and making head space. Call it handing it over to a higher power or God. If you go out 'flustered' then you will be in trouble on the pitch.

'I never said much in the dressing-room, as all you can do is confuse people. The key work was in the training during the week… not the dressing-room the afternoon of the match.'

The standout duels for Seán's Meath team were against Dublin, but he does not dwell on a rivalry which was both fierce and consuming. 'It was an amazing time. No pressure. We had earned the right to be there. Everything was left on the field. We have developed many good friendships. We had amazing times in sport both in defeats and victories'.

Meath's Leinster final win over Dublin in 1986 was the big breakthrough of the Boylan era. He had created a 'spirit' within the team, a bond, a togetherness, and from this success flowed. Seán insists he is of a naturally shy disposition, and that this characteristic afforded him a turning point in his management of Meath. He began to foster a different culture at team meetings. It was about openness and honesty. He introduced a circle of discussion, and he began to properly emphasise the importance of players taking individual responsibility for what they were part of, both for themselves and for the team.

'That's the code,' he insists. 'That's the only way it can be. We trained together… we ate together; yet so many of the lads were so diverse, their views were so different. But when they came together, they came as Meath men.'

He recalls the epic four-game series with Dublin at the beginning of the 1991

Bringing Yourself
to the Battle

SEAN WAS DIAGNOSED with prostate cancer in 2009 and the illness recurred four years later.

'I marvel at the great oncologists who do such great work... it's not just a job to them. And the Marie Keating Foundation do such great work. They have helped so many people get it off their chest which is vital as the patient perspective and experience is so important.

'There are also people doing great work in research and treatments are improving all the time. I am one of the lucky ones that came through this experience and it is a powerful place to be. I have great vitality and great energy now.

'I would tell someone who is newly diagnosed not to be afraid to ask questions... and also to believe in themselves. Modern medicine does amazing things... but you have to be ready to put in some of your own stuff to the battle as well.'

•••

Leinster Championship. 'Suddenly this contest caught the imagination of a nation that had just come through the euphoria of the World Cup adventure in Italia '90. In the wake of that tournament, gaelic games were perceived to be almost dead... and then these amazing four games came along. They were very physical games, powerful football played with unrelenting intensity.'

Seán finally retired from his position as manager of the Meath team on the evening of August 31, 2005, after over two decades in charge. During his time with Meath, he managed the team to four All-Ireland Championships (1987, '88, '96 and '99), three National League titles and eight Leinster Championships.

Seán concludes that he was just asked to do his best. 'I was never any greater that the man who carried the bags. I was never fortunate enough to play in an All-Ireland final, but I was lucky enough to manage teams in seven finals. I just thank God for the talents and people who were given to me... and that I had an opportunity to work with those talents.'

He was conferred as Freeman of the County of Meath on April 23, 2006, and he was later entered into the GAA Hall of Fame for his services to Meath football.

The Herbalist

Herbalists are part of ancient cultures. It is to Tara that Seán Boylan traces his herbalist roots, all the way back to the tumultuous year of 1798. His great great grandfather came from Tara to Dunboyne at that time with four of the 'original remedies of Tara', and 217 years later, Seán carries on his ancestors' work at the impressive Dunboyne Herbal Clinic, just outside the small town close to the border with County Dublin.

He is the fifth generation in his family in Dunboyne working with herbs. He defines himself as such. 'This is who I am. I am not a doctor... I am a traditional herbalist.

'For generations, people came up to our house for a cure. People came to us for cures for osteoporosis arthritis... there was no cure, but herbs were local to the area. There was another cure for tuberculosis. Dropsy was another one we had. As kids, people called to our house for the cure. Also, we grew our own herbs.

'All the illnesses would have been local and so also were the cures! What I do, developed from there. Some of the herbs we work with predate medicine; some are from the 16th century and can even can be traced to Skellig Michael in the 10th century. I started with my dad when I was 17. My dad believed... and he was able to use some of his cures to sustain a long life. Today people want to know what is in it, in our cures? What I inherited is an art form which has become a science. But it has *always* been a science.'

Seán talks more about Tara and the ancient Kings of Ireland. 'The energy in the place!' he exclaims, as he reflects on one of the most affecting places in his native county. Regularly, he took his Meath teams to train on the Hill of Tara, as well as the sea at Bettystown, but he believed Tara gave his players a sense of sacred ground. It was about the history, the heritage... a *meaning* that surrounded them

Today, Seán has six children with Tina, née Yeats, a native of Dunboyne, whose family have known the Boylan family for generations

Tina had worked at the Boylan farm for years when she was young, and during that time she became very close to Seán's late mother Gertie, and to Seán himself. They were 'just great pals' until one day in the summer of 1990, when Tina expressed reservations about moving to Australia to work as a nurse. Seán offered her an alternative.

'I just said to her, "Sure maybe you can hang around a bit... you might hang around with me?" With that the doorbell rang. It was one of the lads who works with me. A neighbour had died; it was two o'clock in the morning and he was really upset, and he called up.

'Two weeks later, I got to meet Tina again and she said, "Were you serious what you said to me?" I told her I was. She said, "Me marry you?"

'I said, "Will you think about it?"

'A few months later, we got engaged, got married... and that was it.'

Maranatha

'Prayer is a huge part of my life,' Seán confides. 'I was in the car recently on a long drive and I spent around 20 minutes reciting the 'Maranatha'... *Come Lord Jesus* mantra. I pray for the ability to do the best and be truthful to what I see.

'If I'm going somewhere, or am asked to speak at a function, I begin with a prayer... often the Memorare or the Serenity Prayer. The rosary beads travel everywhere with me too!'

Seán's faith was never pushed on anybody. 'Some of the lads were so deep in their faith. They might have questions about the Church as an institution, but they have a very reflective faith.'

Seán continues to reflect on who he is, and what he has become. 'I know little about myself. I am still learning and reflecting on my life. I am grateful for God's mercy. I am lucky, being married to Tina and having six children. My family are all different ages, and that is the mystery of life.'

He believes God's hand guided his dad, and subsequently himself through life. He attests that his mother's prayers to Our Lady have become his prayers too, but with a special devotion to the Memorare.

Looking back on his career, he reflects that all his endeavours were a labour of love. His love of sport was pure passion.

'No matter which way it went, love was at the heart of it all.

'My lesson is... always be prepared for things to be different from what you expect. I pray for the ability to do the best... and be truthful to what I see.'

●●●

'I went to Mass every Sunday in my youth, which was something of a requirement, and it was only in my early 20s that I experimented by going to Mass regularly before a game. I found that it led me to have a greater sense of peace of mind and relaxed me.'

tony óg regan

HURLER

THE HIGHS AND lows of sport have visited Tony Óg Regan in his life. He is now an experienced performance and well-being coach enabling individuals, teams and organisations unlock the next level of health, well-being, and performance through evidence and research-based practices. Tony has spent over 15 years assisting sporting and corporate teams to maximize performance.

He grew up in Boleybeg on the outskirts of Galway with his parents Tony and Jennifer, and his two sisters Susan and Lisa. He was playing hurling from six years of age for his local club Rahoon-Newcastle. He also played gaelic football with Salthill. His father was a well-known Roscommon inter-county footballer, but moved to college in Galway and subsequently became Director of Sport at NUIG.

'I got a great introduction to sport by going into watch things in NUIG. We only ever went to GAA clubs… all my other sports were played in the garden!

'I had a huge interest in learning at school,' he admits, with a particular love for business and maths. 'I went to Mass every Sunday in my youth, which was something of a requirement, and it was only in my early 20s that I experimented by going to Mass regularly before a game. I found that it led me to have a greater sense of peace of mind and relaxed me.

'It helped to detach me from the game later in the day. It also allowed me to

49

develop a relationship with God. This ritual took on a deep importance in my life and how I prepared for games.'

Going to Mass, he notes, most likely stemmed from an anxiety about his upcoming match and his personal performance. Being in church helped to centre and ground him. 'As a young man it was going to church that gave me peace of mind. The silence and solitude were important for me. No one asks you questions. You are just yourself.

'Being able to sit in silence with your thoughts and prayers, and even reading the scriptures gave me a word or a phrase that would resonate with me at that time and at that moment.'

'When we had an away game, we had a priest on the team bus. In 2005, when I got to my first senior All-Ireland, I recall Mass in the hotel on the morning of a match. This happened with underage teams too. It just was part of our GAA inter-county team preparation. From the age of around 15 it was part of the pre-match ritual.'

Tony also acknowledges that when he had a home game it was important for him to go to Mass on the Sunday morning, and at times even the day before on Saturdays. It was his personal way of preparing. 'Prayer and meditative practice helped to ground me on the weekend of games.

'I had a team member and a close friend Damian Hayes, who lost his brother Keith in an horrific car accident very close to his home. For him he was very conscious of praying before a game, saying a prayer to Keith at his grave the morning of big games. For Damien, his hurling was a way of celebrating and honouring his brother, who played inter-country hurling up to minor level for Galway. He often carried a bottle of holy water in his kit bag. At times he shared one with me too.

'We talked about faith, and the importance of family especially, on bus trips to matches.

'For the bigger games, my mam would sew in a miraculous medal into my togs. That meant a lot... knowing, win or lose, you still had your family with you. It eased the pressure of the day and gave me a groundedness.

'Hurling gave me a connection to my teammates and my community. An opportunity to serve a cause greater than yourself. The enjoyment of trying to master the ball in a game or training situation is very enjoyable. The physical and mental challenges that playing provides has helped me have the confidence to take on different challenges and changes in my life. It gave me confidence as a person.

'And being part of a team instilled great values in me... like teamwork, communication, commitment, resilience, and leadership, to name a few. Even when I went to secondary school, I knew no one when I arrived but through my sport, I got to know 30 other players in no time. This gave me a confidence amongst my peers, allowing me to fit in and belong.

'I don't think I was born with natural talent; it was something that I worked very hard on. I had a passion for it from an early age and, combining this with practice, over time and in the right environment of players and coaches I steadily improved season by season. It was very fulfilling doing things well in training and games, and feeding off the encouragement.'

Dealing with Setbacks

'Throughout life, changes to things that we are used to being a certain way can affect us. Some of the major changes in life that have affected me to varying degrees have been the loss of my grandparents, changing from a small primary school to a massive secondary school, moving from college to full-time work, losing teammates and club members through suicide, losing my county career at 29 and leaving an accountancy career after 10 years to start my own business.

'In college it was harder to find a balance between full-time study, part-time work and training. This got even harder when I was an apprentice accountant... with the amount of time taken up both mentally and physically trying to be your best at sport, and performing at work. I struggled to integrate this life and this led me to fail exams at various times. I ended up under-performing at work and on the pitch, because I did not have the right balance. My mental health was affected during this time. I really struggled.

'In 2008, I went through changes as an athlete by getting dropped from the Galway senior hurling panel in November. I was 24 years old. I had given six years to the senior team (and six as an underage player) and had competed in an All-Ireland final in every age group. Every summer preparing for All-Ireland campaigns was what my mind, body and lifestyle had been conditioned to.'

Don't Lie Down

"**I** DON'T SAY this lightly, but the grief of being dropped is akin to having a loved one leave you. That grief you feel at having your whole world taken away is traumatic,' admitted Tony Óg Regan when interviewed by RTE's Damien Lawlor for his book 'When the World Stops Watching.'

His message?

'Don't let someone dictate your own future. Don't lie down if you feel there's more in the tank. Get on the road you feel is the right one and stay the course. Stay focused. Keep the goals in mind every day. Shit does happen but you can still change things.'

O'Regan stresses the importance of developing other interests outside the bubble of the 'team' and the 'performance'. When he took a complete break from club hurling he simply could not get over the free time at his disposal; time he redirected towards family and friends. Some evenings he ran, sometimes he choose to go out on a lake rowing. He cycled too.

Balance is his bible.

'As a sports psychologist, I am always looking for lights flashing when I talk to athletes. Are they over-absorbed in sport?

'What are their hobbies? If they can't name one... a red flag is raised.'

•••

In March 2009, his contract finished as a trainee accountant. He subsequently was out of a job as an unqualified accountant, and ended up having to repeat his exams.

He went touring Australia for a while to get a break. It was on his return that Tony discovered he was dropped from the team, and that his contract at work was not going to be extended. His mother offered wise advice, suggesting he take a break to press 'pause' and do things for himself... stop trying to be all things at once simultaneously.

'I had put seven-and-a-half years into becoming qualified and had fallen short. For a few weeks, I sat in denial about what happened. The story I was telling myself was one of blame and denial: the manager will surely call me back in before the league, or someone will ring me with a job offer. I felt angry about how I was treated by the manager, county board and my teammates. I felt angry at my boss for not giving me a six-month contract to finish my exams out and get qualified.

'I moved back home and felt helpless and hopeless for a while. No job to get up for, no money coming in... the start of a recession. No county career, and no exams until August.

'I was feeling a real sense of hopelessness. I was focusing on all the imperfections in my life. I was blaming everything outside of me and not taking responsibility for my life.'

He was dropped from the county squad at the age of 24 because he was not performing to the set targets. 'I didn't get a lot of my life right around this time... my personal relationships, my passion for sport, my career... none were working well at this time of my life.

'I was putting too much pressure on myself with my hurling to the extent that it all fell apart. This was a very low year for me.'

Reconnect and Rebuild

Gradually he took this period in his life to reconnect with himself. He read, studied, trained, and took the time to do what was necessary to rebuild his relationships. Things took a new turn after he passed his exams and also ended back on the Galway team.

Twelve months later he had a job. He knew, now, it was doubly crucial to focus on balancing all that was important in his life.

Tony admits that he had to dig deep to refocus his life. 'I went to prayer most days and attending Mass weekly and at times during the week. I found this a grounding for me at this time. This was part of my recovery and finding my purpose. When I did this, I knew God was looking after me.'

He learned that after it (sport and career) was all taken away from him, 'I would not tie all my happiness into this again. I am my own man outside of sport. I have a lot more to offer the world outside of my hurling. I have other potentials to realise.

'I was not going to put all my hopes, happiness and dreams into hurling, because when I did, and it did not work out, I felt like I was no good as a person at times in my head. When I came back to it, I knew I would enjoy it more within a wider perspective on what really matters in life.'

After his return, he found the next few years were probably his best in a Galway jersey. He was named as vice-captain, and was nominated for two All Stars, and won a Leinster senior title and National League medal. 'I came close to an All-Ireland medal too. I am proud of this second chapter of my career, in how I came back from set-backs and adversity to learn to love myself and the game in a new way.'

To keep his life in context, Tony has acquired a few skills to assist him. 'Every time I journal, I know I am communicating with something higher than myself. Every time I practice meditation it is me speaking to a higher intelligence, whether that is God or whatever, or something greater... I think there is something out there in the spiritual world that guides us all.'

He has no real memories of religious moments in the dressing-room. Tony would say a private prayer himself before a match, not to win but, 'just to play well and for everyone to do their best. Generally, it was an *Our Father* and *Hail Mary*... never to win!'

After the match? 'If I was at Mass I could reflect on what happened at a distance. It was a moment of thanks.'

His sporting journey, he states, has made him a more rounded and reflective person. He has no regrets. For him it was not a sacrifice. 'Absolutely not a sacrifice. I have been fortunate to have been able to do what I did. I feel privileged to meet the people I have met and perform at the levels I have. Coming from the age of six to play in national finals at every age group in the best stadiums, with some of the best players. This has been a privilege.'

His memories of walking out onto the pitch of Croke Park in front of 82,000 people live with him still, and forever. 'That is a very spiritual feeling, coming out onto the pitch at 21 years of age and hearing the synchronicity of noise from that number of people... that is one amazing energy coming at you and into you. It takes a minute to focus and get back to doing what you are there to do.'

The Next Steps

Tony stopped at 29 playing inter-county for Galway. It was not his decision; he would like to have kept going. He continues to play in his local club and still enjoys the game after 20 years on the senior team. 'I love to see younger members come through on to the team and I like to be able to help them as a mentor. It is my responsibility to be a leader and role model, to show them how to act on and off the field.

'In my final year in school I was a prefect. It was a responsibility I took seriously. It is important for me to look out for all members of the team. I like to help them. That's what helped me when I got onto the senior team... others looking out for me. I am just giving back.' He is now vice-chairman of his local club Rahoon/Newcastle.

While his county career was ending, Tony undertook further studies in Sport and Exercise Psychology and Executive Coaching. This has led him to discover the benefits of mental skills training to improve health, well-being and performance.

He subsequently set up his own business to help individuals and teams achieve peak performance in life, in business and in sporting pursuits. He admits that he feels like he has received the hand of God through some of the people who have helped him in his life.

'Some coaches have guided and protected me with their support. Some of these people have helped me to find my path in life.'

He may have the unfulfilled dream of missing out on winning an All-Ireland with his county, but Tony still has more dreams. 'I'd love to win a county and All-Ireland championship with my club. I want to have as many happy and healthy relationships and memories in my life as possible. I want to be a great husband, a great father in time and a friend to those I meet.'

He would like to be remembered as someone who was honest, kind and inspiring. 'If I can show up each day living these values and trying to help others in fulfilling their potential, that will be success for me.'

●●●

'The five S's of sports training are stamina, speed, strength, skill and spirit, but the greatest of these is spirit.'

— Ken Doherty

US Decathlon Champion,
Track and Field Coach
(1905-1996)

'I am not sure why, maybe it's just a phase
in my life. I do reflect on the doctrines
of the Church and am working out my
opinions. However, I may not devote like
others, and may drift in and out of my
spiritual life. It is something that I may
come back to. It's not huge in my life at
present, but I am open to it in the future.'

niamh cotter

GAELIC FOOTBALLER

NIAMH COTTER HAS had big choices in her young life. From Glengarriff, a small village in West Cork, she plays for the Beara club. In her teens, she was extensively committed to playing basketball, athletics and ladies football. She attended Coláiste Pobail Bheanntraí which provided her the foundations for her athletics career and coming second in the All-Ireland 3,000 metres helped to spark interest in the US, where Notre Dame signalled their interest. 'When I was in secondary school athletics was my primary focus. I was lucky as I have a natural ability to be aerobically fit.'

She has always had an aptitude for sport. 'It is the biggest passion that I have had from a young age. I kicked a ball before I could walk!' Initially she played football and then basketball, before excelling at athletics. 'I won a few nationals and made a few national squads. I focussed on long distance… 3,000 metres and cross-county. I was balancing serious athletics with basketball… and then eventually I made the Cork minor football team.'

She decided to commit to playing football in Cork as she was part of the Cork minor panel. She liked being part of a team rather than the solitary sport of athletics. 'When I got to around 17, I had to make a decision. I was considering the possibility of a scholarship in Notre Dame. This was the same year I made the Cork minor team, so that opened my eyes to many opportunities.

'I found athletics quite lonely. In team sports I had other people, friends... a little community of people. In Bantry, I was the only girl of my age running. The training was tough on your own. I loved it. However, I loved the camaraderie of team sport with football and basketball. That ethos was more suited to my personality. That was the big factor.

'I was playing club football with Glengarriff, basketball in Bantry... and running also! My dilemma was either football and basketball, or athletics. In the end, I choose football! I went with the team sports. I went to college in UCC and played basketball with UCC also. I made the O'Connor Cup squad, which is an intervarsity competition. By virtue of that, I was called into the Cork senior team. Eventually, I had to take a step back from basketball to focus on my studies.'

Her parents are local doctors, and she has a brother and sister. Even though still a young woman playing sport and taking the first steps in a career in law herself, Niamh has won an All-Ireland medal playing with Cork ladies when she was part of the extended panel in 2016.

As part of her degree, she had to take Erasmus last year, and Niamh chose Université de Montréal. On her return, she went on to do further studies in Dublin. 'I studied International Law as an undergraduate and followed it up with an MA in European Law. Both were demanding courses. I couldn't fit it all in. When I got the call up to the senior team, I dropped down a division in basketball... I just could not commit to basketball. There are many transferables in sport. I was drawn to the team sport and the friendships of winning and losing together.'

After starting a Masters in European Law at UCD Niamh switched to play her club football in Dublin with Kilmacud Crokes. A key part of her decision was that the eight-hour round trip to West Cork wasn't feasible. Once the exams were over, she began work as a trainee solicitor in a corporate law firm in Dublin. There was not much free time in her schedule at this point.

'It's over five hours for me to get home to Beara from Dublin,' she explains. 'It's one thing going down to Cork for training, but I am only halfway home at that point. It was a very hard decision to make, to be honest. I had put it off, but I spoke to a few people about it and you have to be a bit realistic about the situation.'

Time away and Timelines

In 2020, she damaged a disc in her back and after it robbed her of eight months of the season, she made it back and played the last 17 minutes of Cork's All-Ireland final defeat to Dublin in 2020.

'I think maybe the one thing I learned from last year is that it's so important to not get too caught up in timelines. I was initially told I'd be back on a pitch in four weeks. Then that went to eight weeks… and then eight months later, I still wasn't back playing.

'I have had a long year of injury. It is amazing that the girls have kept in touch and check in with me. They could have moved on and focused on themselves. I value their messages of support and reaching out. That has reaffirmed me in team sport. They are lifting me through the lows! It is a like a second family. You can get similar support in athletics, but not to the same extent. With athletics being a solo sport, it can be more of a lonely journey.'

She has also had time to reflect as she watched the Tokyo Olympics in 2021, and wondered what if she had stayed with her athletics career

'It is interesting to reflect that the three girls representing Ireland in the Tokyo Olympics all would have been running when I was competing. It was a case of… what if! I came to a realisation in athletics that because of my times, I may not make it outside of Ireland. Yet I also knew I could achieve success with football. A compromise for the better.'

Niamh has learned to reflect deeper on the meaning of her life also. 'I have always been Niamh the runner/footballer. My identity has been assumed into Niamh the sportsperson. Now I have spent a lot of time reflecting on who I am really. My injury has forced me to separate my identity from sport. I am now trying to discover other things about myself.' She is also very appreciative of the support that she has been given by her friends as her recovery approached the two-year mark.

'I have learned I am probably more academic than I realised. I enjoy learning. I am really interested in the human rights side of law. I have a new sense of social justice. I have definitely engaged with this more these past 18 months. I have a natural interest in social justice and law. It most likely comes from my parents. They have worked overseas as doctors. They have passed that sense of helping

Viewing Herself

'MAYBE IT IS a time to get to know myself... rather than me and sport,' Niamh reflects on her long running injuries. 'There is more to me and more that I am passionate about... it's not just sport. I am now reading more, listening to podcasts. I am fostering the friendships I have and if I was playing sport, I would not get to deepen these experiences.

'I tied my identity too much to sport. Winning and losing also impacted how I viewed myself. I have learned now how to separate myself from my sport.' She would like to be identified and remembered for 'who I am and not what I did'.

•••

those less well off. All my siblings have this.' She recalls a story about a time when she was watching Cork play. Her mind drifted towards the reality that in some countries girls and women cannot play sport.

Niamh also demonstrated a deep sense of self-awareness and thankfulness for her chance to play sport. 'We are so fortunate as girls who can play sport, unlike some countries in the world. I have been able to study again... in some countries girls cannot do that.'

The Young Niamh

'I come from a family where we attend Mass at weekends. In primary school, I also was an altar server and was involved in local parish life. Gradually, as older teenagers, I drifted from the regular practice of faith.

'At home, we have traditions, such as gathering around the crib at Christmas, and we would pray. Dad would also remind us to pray for people who are sick or dying. We were allowed the flexibility to practice our faith at a certain age. I do pray, but not in a regular way like my parents... for me it is more occasional. That might return.

'I am not sure why, maybe it's just a phase in my life. I do reflect on the doctrines of the Church and am working out my opinions. However, I may not devote like others, and may drift in and out of my spiritual life. It is something that I may come back to. It's not huge in my life at present, but I am open to it in the future.'

Niamh is also realising how her understanding of faith has overlaps with her passion for law, and social justice and fairness. 'There are a lot of principles of faith that come into my understanding of law. The 'love one another' teaching is one that I try to have in my life. I appreciate the role of forgiveness. I try to apply them to my life and abide by them.'

Like other young adults of a similar age, Niamh hasn't really had deep meaningful conversations about God or faith. She does recall small rituals around sport. 'Going off to a match my parents might throw holy water on me!' This is something she hadn't thought of in a while. She also remembers that she, 'saw a few bottles of holy water in kit bags!'

Another feature of playing inter-country sport were the traditions of a final.

'Before some big games, such as the All-Ireland in 2016, we had a Mass before the game. This was a tradition with the girls gathering for Mass the evening before. Fr Kelleher said the Mass. For me, my memory of this was that it was a special moment in time. Being together and being in silence was very profound and calm for me. We also had this in 2017 in the O'Connor final; some of us went to Mass in Mayo in a village and the local priest noticed us and welcomed us.'

When she was injured, she points out that she didn't pray. 'I am not in touch with my faith but I have much food for thought. The Christian principles are very relevant to me.

'Being injured is a tough journey. As the months go on, I have learned how to deal with it. I have also just started work, so in a change from studying I have less time to think about myself. I now can throw myself into other things.'

Looking to the Future

'There is a question as to whether I get back to sport. I hope so. I was not enjoying it when I played. I took it for granted, getting anxious before games. Now I have a perspective. I will return a different person. I will enjoy and give thanks for every moment of future sport. I am now throwing myself into other projects such as my solicitor exams.

'I want to remain occupied and use my time in a more fruitful way. I will always be involved in sport, but there are many factors now in play, especially the appreciation for being able to play. Also, the girls keeping in touch… this is the 'love one another' faith in action.' She has since passed her college exams and has commenced her training as a solicitor.

'I'd like to be remembered as the person who was always there for other people and looked out for other people, and made sure people were doing okay. When everything is taken away, what do you do? You learn about your character. I like to think I am more resilient now because of the obstacles that I have faced.

'Taking a step back helps me learn how to be a better person, who can make a difference. I really do hope that I can be remembered as 'a good friend'.

●●●

'The secret of my success over the 400 metres is that I run the first 200 metres as hard as I can. Then, for the second 200 metres, with God's help, I run harder.'

— Eric Liddell

Runner from Scotland in the 1920's and 30's
and Olympic Gold Medallist

'I am not perfect, but I am trying hard.
I learned that going out onto the field I
offered everything to God. Whatever the
outcome! You hand over fear and failure to
God. This gives a freedom and allows you
to express yourself more.'

ger brennan

GAELIC FOOTBALLER

GER BRENNAN IS a gaelic footballer of renown, who has won an All-Ireland title with his club St Vincent's and was the resolute No.6 on the Dublin team which claimed a landmark All-Ireland victory in a sensational late comeback against Kerry in 2011.

As a younger man, he graduated from Maynooth College with Undergraduate and Master's Degrees. He qualified as a schoolteacher, and taught Irish and religion at St Kevin's College, on Ballygall Road in Dublin. In November 2015, he was appointed Gaelic Games Executive at University College Dublin.

From a family of nine, Ger grew up on Dublin's north inner city, just off Dorset Street. For him growing up consisted of a mix of being involved in the local community, going to a local school and an involvement in his local parish of Gardiner Street, a famous Jesuit parish.

'Faith and church was something that was very normal for me. I was an altar server at Mass, and I attended parish youth clubs, and Music Makers... a youth group where we learned to play music. I even played guitar in the Gardiner Street Gospel Choir. I was engaged with the Church from an early age, going to Mass on Saturday evenings and Sunday mornings. The Jesuits had a huge influence on me.'

Some of his earliest 'holy' memories are of going to Mass with his parents. 'If you were bold, you were brought closer to sit with my da! To keep a check on me! I wasn't always sure what was going on, but I valued the silence… the chance to be still. It was a great tool that my parents instilled in me, going to Mass every Sunday as a family. The church was a place of fun, and offered all the options that the parish had for young people.'

His parents were great supporters of their Jesuit parish. Ger grew up hugely influenced by the local parish and his involvement in it. The parish had many local outreaches to keep young people involved in the community, as the Jesuits were very much involved in the local community.

'Brother Eamon Davis and Tom Phelan SJ had a huge influence on my family. And Brother Tom and Bridie Ash in the Music Makers… the work they did taught us more than just holy and secular music, they brought us on trips out of the city… to Mosney (a residential camp) and mountain climbing. I remember lots of real active communal fun. I was part of that life until I was 18, and I played guitar in the gospel choir until my early 20s. I even played in Vicar St, the Olympia and the National Concert Hall with the gospel choir.'

Jesuit Influences

Ger attended Belvedere College on a scholarship programme. At Belvedere he played rugby, and football, while keeping up hurling and gaelic football with St Vincent's GAA club.

He admits to having the same struggles with his faith that many teenagers went through. At school, through the influence and ethos of the Jesuits, he had learned the lesson of, 'Trying to be a man for others, to use your talents and be a light in the world and to bring other people with you'. These are values embedded by the founder of the Jesuits, St Ignatius of Loyola.

He learned how to integrate one of the Jesuit prayer technics into his life… the Examen. This helps us to look at God in our life, every day. This helped Ger at times of 'spiritual desolation'. He never lost his faith, but he had big questions as he struggled to integrate his maturing faith into a life as a teenage and, subsequently, a young adult.

Belvedere also had a Social Diversity programme where nearly fifteen percent attending are scholarship children from socially challenged environments. Padraig

Madden, one of the teachers, oversaw this and he was a huge support to Ger. Another positive influence was Fr Jim Culliton who looked after the junior cycle.

'In school, what I recall is the sense that you belong, God loves you... and also the Jesuit motto *AMDG*... *For the Greater Glory of God* really impacted on me, my understanding that my gifts and talents were for the service of others. This value has impacted and stayed with me. It instilled in me a sense of justice and fairness.'

The school ethos resonated with values his parents had passed on, including that of gratitude. He is grateful for this positive influence. He was also taught not to feel sorry for oneself and be resilient... and just 'get on with it'. These were family values that he hopes to pass on to his new family.

He learned Irish in school with his teacher, Micheál Ó Murchú! 'He was from Donegal and brought us to Gweedore, to the Gaeltacht!' There, Ger fell in love with the language and the culture... sport, people... and the women! 'He taught us if you're speaking English, what a pity... say it in IRISH.'

Role of Sport

Ger comes from a very sporting family, but a family which was predominantly made up of soccer people.

His uncle Fran had played for Ireland, and lined out for Shelbourne, Dundalk. The family followed local teams Belvedere FC and Shelbourne, even though Bohemians FC was closer to their home.

'There were very few GAA pitches locally,' Ger recalls. 'Many of my friends went to school in St Vincent's and played with the local club. Others went to Coláiste Mhuire, just off Parnell Square... and I played a few games for them as a non-registered player too!'

Initially, his gaelic football career commenced with Na Fianna on Mobhi Road, and it was only later, when he was 15, that he joined St Vincent's. He joined the club – most deeply-rooted in Dublin GAA culture, and famously the home of Dublin legend Kevin Heffernan – because they were so good at underage. 'At Na Fianna we got beaten a lot.' Though, at the same time, Ger retains fond memories of his early days in the club, and the volunteers who steered him along the right path and saw to it that he had the opportunity to begin an underage career in the famous sky blue of Dublin.

Digging Deeper

IT WAS PAT Gilroy and Mickey Whelan who asked the Dublin footballers to look at themselves, and look deeper still. The result was a thrilling breakthrough win, 1-12 to 1-11, over Kerry in the 2011 All-Ireland final.

'It was hard work though,' Ger remembered in 'Game of my Life', written by David Sheehan. 'My God, the training was tough. The 6am sessions are all the rage now, but they were new at the time. The 6am stuff started with Vincent's, which helped us to win the club All-Ireland. I found myself going to bed around 9 or 10pm... because you're up at 5am for the 6am session.

'But then you're overthinking things... afraid you're going to sleep in. Then, you can't sleep and the next thing... it's half one or two in the morning! For the first few weeks of those early morning sessions, I'd say fellas had feck all sleep. Physiologically, from a sports point of view, I'd say those sessions made very little sense.

'However, I'd say that the psychological element was at the core of it. I'm not sure I'd say it was 90%/10% in terms of the psychological/physical split, but it wouldn't be far off that. I enjoyed it though. You're 25... I think I'd just started teaching... life was handy, I was paying my rent and I wasn't spending too much money on anything else because all I was doing was sleeping, eating and training.

'Some mornings were harder than others, but the mornings that you're not in the humour, the energy of the collective feeds you. That's the beauty of team sport.'

•••

Sport and Faith

Travelling to matches on the team bus, or rooming with different teammates, Ger has always found an opportunity to talk about his faith.

'I was a tough, aggressive player, and I was often asked by other lads on the team, how can you play the way you play and yet you are into God? For me these were opportunities to contextualise what I am about, and make it relevant for the other people I played with. Going to Mass, when we travelled around the country with the team, was great and many local priests would welcome us and give us a mention. Each man on the team attended Mass for personal reasons; it was a personal choice to attend, there was no pressure on anyone on the team to go.'

Conversations on the team bus might gravitate to his work, his study of theology, chaplaincy and God. He recalls great conversations about God, Church, and faith. 'It was always something I was comfortable talking about. I never imposed my beliefs on anyone. You propose… not impose. It is never about forcing people to believe what I believe.'

But prayer, to Ger, always helped. He prayed before games, which he says led him to a place of peace. At the same time, Ger stresses that he is not a 'Holy Joe', noting that there were times he drifted like any 20-year-old. He notes that he was in Dingle one weekend on a break. He visited a local church for some personal time and prayed before the Blessed Sacrament, and he remembers being drawn back into a deeper relationship with God.

'I remember one Christmas morning we all went to Mass, then visited the graveyard. When we came home I went for a run along the canal, near Croke Park. I knew that this extra bit of training was important, as my nearest competitor on the Dublin team wouldn't be training on Christmas day. This was my determination and sole focus. To be the best in my position!'

Sacrifice, Routine and Ritual

Dublin's breakthrough All-Ireland victory in recent times was crafted by the management team of Pat Gilroy and Mickey Whelan, two other St Vincent's men and close friends. Gilroy and Whelan built a powerful resilience amongst the players in their dressing-room, Ger states. 'They instilled in us the value and privilege of representing our county. They reminded us of the huge sacrifice people around us were also making, to allow us the opportunity of being the best we could be in the Dublin jersey... our families, our work colleagues.

'When we were knackered, we found that we could draw strength from what we were doing.... remind ourselves that what we were doing was a pleasure, even if training was brutally tough on a particular day. In a weird way the brotherhood and fraternity was something amazing, without even winning an All-Ireland.'

Not everyone in the Dublin dressing-room followed the same pre-match rituals. Some players listened to music, others went onto the stand to watch the pre-match build up. 'I used to listen to Christian music on my playlist on my earphones. That ritual was important to me.'

After St Vincent's, also coached by Mickey Whelan at the time, won the All-Ireland Club Championship in 2008, Ger went home after the match and had a moment of quiet contemplation. He read from his mother's bible... Psalm 65... *Only in God is my soul at rest.* He read that passage for a long time. He then went to the St Vincent's clubhouse in Marino, and let his hair down, celebrating with his teammates.

'We won the club final in Croke Park in 2008, but walking back onto the pitch four years later, in 2011, in front of 80,000 people... that was the culmination of a life's ambition as a gaelic footballer. To play in front of a full stadium... running out and waiting... the energy is just electric.

'I am full of life, and full of gratitude at a time like that. Five minutes before I go out onto the field, I have a moment. I spend that moment in a private prayer of gratitude. My seat was in the corner of the dressing-room. My mind wanders towards that Jesuit motto, AMDG... Ad Majorem Dei gloriam *(For the Greater Glory of God).*

'I pray for the safety of all players... and pray for no serious injuries! We all shake hands at the end of every game, we all need to walk away from the stadium.'

Inspiration

One of the role models in sport that Ger looked to for inspiration was Dessie Farrell, the former All-Ireland winner in 1995 and present manager of the Dublin senior football team. He was given a copy of Dessie's autobiography, *Tangled up in Blue*. 'His story instilled in me a dream and a hope that that could be me... winning an All-Ireland. Whilst Dessie had a personal life of challenge, he was ahead of me in school and in the club (in Na Fianna). He was someone to look up to, as a role model and a footballer. I got to know him later, and he really sees the person in sport, not just the sportsperson.'

Later in his career, Ger appeared on television, on the Irish edition of the quiz *Mastermind* and his chosen topic was the Life of Ignatius of Loyola, much to the surprise of other contestants. Little did they know that Ger has always looked towards St Ignatius of Loyola, not just in prayer, but also as a form of inspiration.

During his college years, he wrote and researched his Thesis on Peter McVerry, the well-known campaigner and Jesuit priest, who is based in Dublin and works with young homeless people. Ger admires people who puts their faith into action.

'I've grown up in an all-male world, yet St Therese of Avila, another mystic, appeals to my contemplative life. She helps me tune into the Lord.'

He deflects success towards, 'gratitude for what God has given you in life...'

Giving Back

At the end of his school years, Ger Brennan thought he would work towards being an engineer. He was due to go to Columbia on a Jesuit programme. In conversation with some of the other people who were going, it came up in conversation about training to be a chaplain. It was an unexpected conversation, which in turn led him to changing his mind and making a leap of faith in a new direction.

'God spoke through them, and more or less told me to change my course. You meet God in people and from people.' As a result, his career path took him into teaching, working in Chaplaincy, and working for a time with the International Eucharistic Congress in 2012, before taking up his current role in UCD.

He is no longer involved in elite sport but it was a huge part of his life, and now remains a central part of his career. Ger is married with two young children, and he explains how he now wants to help pass on these values he learned and inherited to his young family. Ger and his wife want to embed a tradition of family prayer, going to church and learning about faith in action.

He is still involved in sport on the college campus in UCD. 'I often notice some of them have rosary beads, or holy water or scapulars.' This can, he says, lead to a very different conversation. 'Some have a prayer and spiritual life, but may have lost the connection to the institutional Church. I am very happy to talk with them about God, about faith and my connection with God... showing young people that God loving them is important.'

God can use sports people, as well as 'holy people' to connect with others. It is a life skill that he has learned, the ability to accompany young people as he was accompanied in his home parish of Gardiner Street. Sports people can also be signposts for others on the spiritual path.

'I am not perfect, but I am trying hard. I learned that going out onto the field I offered everything to God. Whatever the outcome! You hand over fear and failure to God. This gives a freedom and allows you to express yourself more.

'I still try to do this today, in my life after elite sport.'

Ger is still on the road to nurturing and deepening his relationship with God. He continues to read different spiritual authors. He recalls a story of going to confession on Campus in UCD, which provided an opportunity to reflect on his life and seek forgiveness for past wrongs. He 'confessed' that it gave him a spiritual fix.

'Once I tune into God, it is a great station to tune into.'

When asked for his potential epitaph, he naturally replies, '*AMDG... For the Greater Glory of God!*'

●●●

STANDING alone

'When I went out on the big races, I just
left it to God with his words, 'Thy will
be done'... it was whatever was God's
will. I had done my preparations, and
I left it in God's hands. If I won or was
beaten, I just was grateful.'

johnny murtagh

JOCKEY AND TRAINER

ONE OF IRELAND'S greatest jockeys, Johnny Murtagh did not take the traditional route through the Sport of Kings, to get to where he is today.

From the small village of Bohermeen in Meath, nestled between Navan and Kells, Johnny quickly explains that his life as a young boy was 'a million miles' removed from the glamorous world of horseracing. His dad was a local builder, and his mum ran the home. Like many other sports achievers, he was totally consumed by participation in every and any sport, and it wasn't until his teenage years that Johnny turned his attention to horse riding. Before then, he had a chance to join Blackburn Rovers in England. The dream of playing gaelic football in the green and gold of Meath was just as strong as the potential life as a professional footballer across the water.

'I didn't like school much, I wasn't a great attender.

'I was always into sport. I was captain of teams in basketball and football. I loved to run. I was into boxing… I was Ireland under-14 champion. So, you see I was always driven to win, and achieve. Yet… I didn't ride a horse until I was 15!'

For him, his route towards horse riding and the parade ring, started in the boxing ring!

'One night I was boxing and a person said to my mother… "Your son would make a good jockey!" He told her that I had good balance… was light, tenacious, brave. My mum wrote to the apprentice school in Kildare.

'My only family connection were a few uncles who went to races and backed horses, just like many other people. As I think back, I do remember writing an essay in school about winning the Grand National because, as a kid, I grew up watching Red Rum in the 1970s and those amazing Grand National races.

'I watched the races with my granny. Red Rum won, lost the following year… and won again. This is the only horse I can remember as a kid.'

Like many other upcoming jockeys, Johnny had to leave home to follow his new dream. His mother wrote to the Racing Academy and Centre of Education (RACE) noting her son had all the attributes needed to be a jockey! He was accepted into RACE in Kildare, which was a training place for apprentice jockeys.

'I left home at 15, went to Kildare and really loved it… living and racing with 26 other lads. I come from a small family so being part of something like this, I really enjoyed it and all the social life… and also the new experiences of hanging out with other lads playing football and going to the cinema!'

For the young jockey, Saturday nights were a big deal, as usually there were no races on Sundays.

The Outsider becomes the Insider

'I love sports, but I am a winner. I just loved winning.'

He describes his arrival at RACE as an apprentice jockey. 'It is an eight-month course and after two months you are sent to a yard to a trainer. I was sent to John Oxx, who was based on The Curragh in Kildare. That's where it started for me… I signed as an apprentice.

'My first ride was on May 8 in the Phoenix Park… my third ride, I won. That was a great year… I rode 12 winners between May and October. I also won the November Handicap at the end of the year. This was a big deal, as it was the last day of the season!'

Johnny was the outsider at first.

He only knew one jockey before he travelled down to Kildare… Lester Piggott.

'I looked up to Mick Kinane and Christy Roche. I didn't have a mentor… I had to do it on my own, but John Oxx was the boss and I answered to him.' This self-determination and resolve would stand to Johnny in the future. Soon, he would be noticed by others throughout the industry.

'I met Tony McCoy on his first ride, and we both recognised each other. People referred to Tony as the new kid on the block.' Johnny, however, kept his inner focus, humorously noting to himself that... *I'm the only kid on the block!*

'I ended up winning that race!' He would go on to win so many races, and by his second year was Champion Apprentice. He was Irish Champion Jockey on five separate occasions, and throughout his glittering career there would be 106 Group winners, and over 3,000 winners in total. However, Johnny still recalls being the 'kid on the block'.

Then, for him, everyone was 'the opposition'.

'I was driven to win. Also, I was driven by the fear that someone could come in and take my position. I did not come from the horse world, so I was an outsider.

'I needed to be on top to avoid being dropped.'

Only the Good go to Heaven

Like any traditional Irish Catholic family, Johnny's parents and grandparents nurtured some of the key foundations of faith. As a young boy he was an altar server and even cut the grass in his local parish. He notes, especially, the influence of his granny and her faith. 'My granny was always religious, and I went to Mass with her on a Sunday. We were not an overly religious house, but we attended Mass.

'My granny was a huge influence on our faith at home. She was the one who instilled faith in us by reminding us to say our prayers.

'Religion, for us, at this time boiled down to... if you are good, you can go to heaven. If not, you were going to hell. It was one of fear. I grew up a little bit fearful in that if I messed up, I would be responsible for it.'

This was not an uncommon understanding of faith in Ireland at that time.

Meanwhile, Johnny continued to pray as he matured as a young jockey. 'I always prayed... especially going past the winning post for a photo finish!

Thy Will be Done

Dealing with success also brought new pressures for a young jockey. At the age of 21, he lost his job after spending eight weeks in St Patrick's Hospital. 'When

I came out,' he observes, 'I had some type of a grasp on the changes I needed to make. I knew I had to change.'

'I got in trouble with drink at the age of 21.

'I ended up in a clinic to try to get some help. I was not in a good space and making a mess of a few things in my life. I went up to St Patrick's in Dublin to talk with Matt Murphy.' He suggested that Johnny give up the drink.

Johnny responded, 'Did you not hear what I am saying? I am under a lot of pressure with the jockeying'. This was the first time I was introduced to Alcoholics Anonymous. That is where my new beginning took place... one day at a time.

'I suppose it took me another 10 years to throw in the towel and take full responsibility.'

Everyone needs a mentor. For Johnny, when he was aged about 30, that came from an encounter with Michael O'Brien from Kildare, who had not 'taken a drink' for 20 years.

'He didn't have much. He wasn't interested in horses... he was interested in me. He was from the town. He was not interested in me as a champion jockey or looking for tips. He wanted to see me do well and to stay off the drink. There was something about him in that he had a 'glow'... something attractive, and something that I wanted.

'He was a very spiritual man. That's where it started for me.'

Johnny began to reassess how he lived his life and reprioritised it. He notes that he moved from just, 'dipping in and out of praying' to being 'grateful to God' for everything he had been given. Giving thanks to God is now central to his philosophy for living.

'I was always grateful to God and my mantra is 'Thank You'.

'I am always giving thanks. I constantly thank Jesus for everything... I do this daily all the time. If I am asked what I am thanking ... my answer is everything! Everything I have... the people I have around me.

'I have great faith. I get up in the morning and it is 'Thy will be done'... not my will. I hand it over to God. I try to go with it daily. Most of the time I don't... but this is how I try to live my life.

'I made a few mistakes in my twenties and in my thirties, but now I have God in my life, who I love, who is looking after me and I just have to keep giving thanks to God. God has made me a positive person. 'This is me now.'

One of Johnny Murtagh's trademark celebrations when he won a race was to look and point up to the sky. His looking up was part of his giving thanks. 'Thy will be done,' became his quiet mission statement for living his life.

'Once I learned how to let go of my mistakes and let go of any guilt I was carrying, that was amazing. Letting go and just waking up each day... a 'new slate'... start again. This was refreshing for me.

'You are judged on what you do today.

'Let go and let God do, that is what I do! I have followed this new start and way of living for 20 years. This is how I live my life today.'

Johnny refocused his life with the realisation that he could take control of it by handing it over to God. This freedom was a liberation that gave him new levels of inner peace and a grateful appreciation of his achievements.

'There is only one person I depend on and that is God. He was minding me all the time and that is why I am very thankful to Him for what He has done in my life. God got me to where I am today. Now it's what I can do for God.

'People can let you down... that's human. I have learnt this the hard way.'

Hearing from Strangers

After Johnny had turned his life around, his colleagues would often slag him in the weigh-room. 'They noticed a difference in me. Jokingly they would ask me to pray for them and I would respond... "Say one yourself, He (God) loves to hear from strangers!"'

He also approached his racing with a different mindset.

'When I went out on the big races, I just left it to God with his words, 'Thy will be done'... it was whatever was God's will. I had done my preparations, and I left it in God's hands. If I won or was beaten, I just was grateful.

'Thy will be done, not mine'

As he got older, he was very much aware of the sacrifices he made for his sport. 'However, the last 10 or so years, I had a better sense of myself and my purpose. I had to watch my weight as a jockey. That was tough. I was getting tired of being hungry... moody, lonely... all connected with the desire to win.

'These were the signs I noticed.'

In 2014, Johnny retired. He was 43.

A Second Life

BELIEF LEFT JOHNNY Murtagh dancing in the rain as he celebrated his first Royal Ascot winner as a trainer. Johnny marked up 48 wins in the saddle at the royal meet, but it was his turn to watch on and cheer as the three-year-old filly bolted home in the Sandringham Stakes.

'Royal Ascot is the best week of the year, it's very special... it's magical,' Johnny remarked after the race. 'And to come back and train a winner now after all those successes as a jockey, I'm just absolutely thrilled. It is probably much tougher being a trainer to get the horses to come to Ascot and to race at their best is very difficult. It's a different feeling altogether... I feel very proud. I feel privileged to be here.

'I feel very proud of my family and the team back home because they put in a lot of work. I have a great team... we are all very close together.'

●●●

'I was ready for it, I knew it... I woke one morning and knew it was time. I spoke to a few folk. I was getting going as a trainer and after some advice, I was ready to retire with no regrets. When you make a decision... don't look back.

'In my decisions, I pray. God directs me.'

Working as a trainer, he hopes that he can serve as an inspiration to young jockeys. 'I am hard but fair. I am trying to get them ready for life and not just on a horse. I try to give them my learned wisdom. I can't tell them to pray, but I do encourage them to have a bit of faith... even a little!'

Johnny continues to try to make a difference in the world of horse racing. He is happy to share his faith. He just wants people to be able to reflect on how they live their own life and maybe they can change things just like him. 'People have told me I am inspirational. It gives them hope and faith! God writes in crooked lines. Religion is for getting people into heaven. Spirituality is for getting heaven into people!

'That's what we need to do as believers!'

He does conclude that God's gentle hand was always in his life, guiding him from rural Meath to the plains of Kildare... to racecourses all over the world. 'God was always there for me. God was there for me in all my life even when I messed things up... God was there. 'God gave me space to follow him!'

Johnny continues to stay connected to his faith and his family still makes time to attend Mass depending on schedules. 'I think it is good to make space. We are not fanatical about going, it's just something we try to do as a family when the time allows. We choose to attend.' His whole family are all involved in sport. Looking back, he acknowledges how grateful he is to God. 'I have great belief and faith in God. God has looked after me, my family, and my kids. I just keep giving thanks to God. I have a lot to be grateful for.'

The roar of the crowd at the finish line still pushes him to do more, of course.

'This is where you want to be, it is your time. I have craved success, and this is where I am meant to be. I have no regrets, as I gave everything the best shot.

'When you are lying in bed, maybe thinking back on the day, if you ask yourself the question... *Have you done your best today?* If you say yes, that's all you need to ask. That's the message I give the young lads. Have no regrets and give your best... be truthful!' For Johnny he will be remembered as one who lived the message... 'The best is yet to come'.

●●●

'Ultimately, you can't argue with someone's personal relationship with God, who is real to them... a relationship which is undeniable. For us it started with someone telling us that a relationship with God is possible.'

katie taylor

BOXER

KATIE TAYLOR HAS been an inspiration to the whole country, but in particular, she has become a brilliant role model for young women. She has shown us all, with her determination and desire, that glass ceilings in sport can be broken. She knew from an early age what she wanted. To be a champion.

'As far back as I can remember, I dreamed of becoming an Olympic champion and I imagined standing on the podium and having the gold medal placed around my neck.'

Growing up in Bray

Katie is deeply attached to where she grew up, in Bray, in Wicklow. She was always playing something; soccer with St Fergal's FC, and gaelic football and camogie for Bray Emmets and Fergal Ogs. She ran with Bray Runners AC. There were so many days when Katie played a combination of her favourite sports, because, to young Katie, it seemed that every sport was her favourite. At the same time, she always believed in winning, and her competitive side was on full display every day she competed. Katie is someone who has broken records and overcame barriers. She played football with a local boys' team. Whilst unusual, she was generally accepted once they saw her competitive side.

Playing a lot of sport with her brothers and training in boxing clubs with boys, Katie believes this made her stronger.

She comes from humble beginnings and says, 'This has me grateful for what we have now'.

Several American colleges were happy to offer her scholarships while she was still studying at St Killian's, however, she opted instead to attend University College Dublin. As her sporting career began to take off, she chose not to complete her studies at UCD.

Katie was a very talented footballer. She played for St Fergal's and Newtown Juniors FC in the Wicklow and District Schoolboys League, honing her skills against the boys. She was widely considered one of the best players in the league, and was a key player on the Wicklow county selection. The Wicklow District League decided to raise the playing age for girls just so Katie could continue to play in the league for a few more years.

During her football career, Katie played ladies football with St Catherine's, Lourdes Celtic, St James' Gate and Peamount in the Dublin area. In 2009, St Catherine's reached the FAI Women's Cup final, but her boxing commitments saw her miss out on the decider itself.

Katie, however, was a member of the Peamount United squad that won the treble – Dublin Women's Soccer League, the DWSL Premier Cup and the FAI Women's Cup – the following season, playing with stars such as Nicola Sinnott, Áine O'Gorman, Sara Lawlor and Louise Quinn. She had already represented the Republic of Ireland women's national team at under–17 and under–19 levels, and would also be capped at senior level. Katie was just 14 when she played for the under-17s, and 15 when she started playing for the under-19s. In one qualifier game for the under-19s, against Macedonia, she hit the net four times.

Katie found that her boxing training aided her football career because it made her physically strong enough to bridge the different age gaps. Between 2006 and '09, she made 11 appearances and scored two goals for the senior team. She made her senior international debut on April 22, 2006 against Switzerland in a FIFA Women's World Cup qualifier at Richmond Park. The Republic of Ireland won 2–0.

'The two sports that I really loved were football and boxing. It was always going to be a showdown between these two. I loved them both and never really wanted to make the decision to drop one or the other. I did manage to avoid making that decision for years and competed in both at an international level well into my twenties.'

Eventually, in 2009, with the London Olympic Games on the horizon, she had to quit international football and concentrate fully on her boxing career. 'Slowly all the other sports that I loved began to be dropped in favour of boxing.'

The Lure of the Ring

Katie's family is steeped in boxing, and her father Pete coached his daughter, and also her two older brothers, Lee and Peter, at St Fergal's Boxing Club, which was set up in a former boathouse in Bray.

But, 'The Sweet Science' was for so long considered not to be an appropriate sport for girls. On occasion, Katie had to put her hair in a net under her helmet to fight boys. Ultimately, her success in the ring would be instrumental in helping to get women's boxing sanctioned in Ireland. In the first officially sanctioned women's fight in Ireland, a 15-year-old Katie beat Alanna Audley from Belfast at the National Stadium.

Christian Values

Katie grew up in a house where Christian values were important, and most of her family attended church locally together. She takes her faith seriously, and she acknowledges that her mother's faith, and her witness, have left a mark on her own life. 'The church provided a wonderful sense of community and belonging,' Katie notes. Going to church, singing a few songs and saying some prayers, she recognises, helped her family.

On Sunday evenings, the family then began to go to St Mark's Church on Pearse Street. 'It was there that my faith and relationship with God really started to grow.' She has described Mark's as one of her favourite places to be for the worship. 'I'm convinced I wouldn't be where I am today without their prayers.'

A deep-rooted, born-again Christianity, nurtured at home and in St Mark's, has been a fundamental part of the Katie Taylor make-up during the years in which she became, firstly, one of the world's most celebrated amateur fighters, and

Katie's Greatest Fight

S HE TRIED TO grin through a swollen face, and she succeeded... just like, against the odds, she had claimed victory in the biggest night of her fight career. Katie had roared back from near defeat and retained her undisputed lightweight championship in May of 2022 with a split-decision win against Amanda Serrano before a sold-out crowd of 19,187 in Madison Square Garden.

'I had to dig deep in there tonight,' she told reporters after. 'This is a special, special moment. The best night of my career for sure. I wasn't sure if anything could reach my Olympic gold medal moment, but tonight was absolutely the best moment of my career.'

In the opening rounds Taylor relied on her superior hand and foot speed to fend off Serrano, and boxed beautifully off the back foot. But Serrano hurt Taylor badly after finally cornering her in the fifth round. She left Katie bloodied, and seemingly exhausted.

'I think I was boxing very, very well in the early rounds and I just got stuck in a fight with her. It's in those moments that the hard work of training pays off. I don't just show courage on fight night. I show courage every single day in training... day after day after day. That's exactly why you train hard, for those moments when you actually are in the trenches.'

•••

finally the most recognised women's professional fighter of all time. And she has made no secret of her love of Christ.

When she refers to Jesus there is no hint of piety or preaching. Her tone doesn't change or shift gears. There is always the sense that she is speaking about something obvious.

She has described her faith as, 'Probably the most important part of my life really. I obviously knew growing up that God had a great plan for my life. Boxing felt like a gift that God has given me, and I want to make the most of this gift and to honour God in everything that I do.

'I have heard people say that boxing isn't a sport that a Christian should become involved in... but, my view is that people who say those things know neither boxing nor the heart of God. I believe that it is God who has given me this talent for boxing.

'I believe this is a gift and that it is my God-given destiny to be a boxer.

'God's promises through the scriptures are relevant to me in how I approach my boxing, but they are also central to my life and who I am.

'He has a plan for me.'

Privacy and Ritual

Katie is a private person who tries to integrate her personal faith into her life. 'My faith is very important to me not just in boxing but in everyday life. I believe God puts dreams and desires in people's hearts. My dream came from God when I was a young girl.

'The only reason I have done great things is that I serve an amazing God. There are no words to describe Him for me... he is the centre of my life. ... I would not be able to step into the ring without God in my life. Anything you need for guidance in your life is in the Bible.

'Mam is my spiritual rock and she is as much a part of my boxing team as anyone else.'

'When I was 17, getting ready for a huge fight, I got a text from my mam to read Psalm 118. While I was reading it the tears were flowing down my face. Everything I needed for that fight was in that psalm. After that fight I read it again... and then before every fight. It became a mantra for me before fights.

'Now, before every fight, my mam comes in to pray with me. That's the most important part of my preparation. It's a real warrior psalm and you get something different from it every time you read it, but every time I read it I realise that it is God who arms me with strength. God gives me the strength in every single fight.

'That psalm never loses its power for me.

Bridget Taylor brushes her daughter's hair, and prays over her. Before the Olympic final in London, in 2012, 'I could sense the emotion in her voice, but she had to hold it together for my sake. This act is perhaps the most important part of my pre-fight ritual. Mam repeated some of Psalm 118 to me, knowing it's one of my favourite pieces from the scriptures. It's the psalm I read when I am away in competition. It is a reminder that it is God that trains my mind for battle... and He is my shield of victory.'

On the day of every fight, Katie follows the same rituals of preparation. 'Throughout the day, I listen to the same worship songs on my iPod and I read the same Bible verses. When I'm boxing or preparing for a fight, that is when I feel closest to God. I have relied on Him and I've put everything in His hands. I've learned from experience that He will never let me down... so I just try to trust him.'

Her focus before a fight is not on the person who is opposing her, but on the God who is standing beside her. She quotes again from scripture... 'No weapon formed against you will prevail, and you will refute every tongue that accuses you. This is the heritage of those that belong to the Lord.'

Katie was the flag bearer for Ireland during the opening ceremony at that 2012 London Olympics, before going on to win gold in the lightweight division.

Hard work was central to Katie's mission to become an Olympic champion, but she also attended the Faith Centre in the Olympic village in London. She was delighted to join other athletes in prayer services which were run by the athletes themselves. For Katie this was a powerful support, knowing that she was joining other Christians in sport talking about how God has helped them.

'I had put pressure on myself and my family to get there, and I had campaigned to get women's boxing into the Olympics. I had been dreaming about winning gold at the Olympic games.'

Even at the end of the final fight, against her Russian opponent Sofya Ochigava, she still tried to balance her anxiety.

'In the final in London, I remember being anxious right until the referee held my arm up as winner. My feelings were supernatural. I dropped to my knees in tears with my arms lifted high above my head.

'I took a moment to close my eyes… and thank God. I tried to take in the accomplishment of a lifetime's ambition and to absorb the noise!'

Speaking on television afterwards, Katie was unafraid to thank God, telling the whole world, 'He (God) is my strength and my shield.' Even in her red boxing robe, she had a verse loaded in her head… 'The Lord is my shepherd and my shield'.

Digging Deep

Of course, like every champion, it has not all been plain sailing for Katie.

Her success in the London Olympics were not followed up with gold in Rio in 2016. After her defeat in the quarter-final, she bravely stated when talking with RTÉ Sport's Joe Stack, 'Sometimes the plans you have in your heart aren't the same as God's plans'.

She has said that the lowest point of her life was that period just after the Olympics in Brazil. But, crucially, Katie knew that she could pick herself up from this low point.

She was at a crossroads in her career.

She also knew that she would have to think long and hard about her next step. 'I had to stand on my own two feet for the first time. It was a tough time for sure, but I knew that moving over to America and starting this new journey… sometimes you must make big sacrifices to make dreams.

'I definitely wouldn't be the person that I am if I didn't have to go through all that.'

Katie is not just credited with raising the profile of women's boxing throughout the world, she is regarded as the outstanding Irish athlete of her generation.

She boldly turned professional, at 30 years of age, in 2016. As an amateur she had won five consecutive medals at the World Championships and six European Championships, and there were many other glorious days in the ring, but the professional fight game was an entirely different proposition.

The six years that followed, however, have been a glorious reign. She has become a two-weight world champion and remains the current undisputed lightweight champion, having held the WBA title since 2017, the IBF title since 2018, and the WBC and WBO titles since 2019. She won the WBO junior-welterweight title in 2019.

Katie is one of only eight boxers (female or male) in the history of the sport to hold all four major world titles – WBA, WBC, IBF and WBO – simultaneously. She was now 'The Greatest', but only Katie Taylor had the ability to take to the greatest stage of all. In April of 2022, she fought and defeated Amanda Serrano in an epic contest, but crucially this was the first time a women's fight headlined the bill at the spiritual home of boxing, New York City's Madison Square Garden.

Putting it all in Perspective

Katie remains determined to be the best she can be. Even if that involves not being conventional in the ways that others are. Her faith will remain core to her values.

'Ultimately, you can't argue with someone's personal relationship with God, who is real to them... a relationship which is undeniable. For us it started with someone telling us that a relationship with God is possible.

'I'm just passing on the good news!'

Katie will be remembered as someone who really has 'fought the good fight'. She continues to remind us all that dreams can come true. The young girl who had dreams of being an Olympian, followed that dream believing and dreaming God's words to Jeremiah.

'For I know the plans I have for you, plans to prosper and not to harm you, plans to give you hope and a future.' (Jeremiah 19:11).

Her dream is not over.

●●●

'For me sport was a religion... with religious sentiment.'

– Pierre de Coubertin

Founder of the International Olympic Committee

'It was a total expression of my faith, recognition of God... and other people, thanking my parents, coaches and everyone who supported me. It was a sense of God's gift to become this one percent of winners in front of the world.'

ronnie delany

ATHLETE

ONE OF IRELAND'S most loved Olympians is the humble, smiling figure of Ronnie Delany. Ronnie journeyed from being an unknown runner, to become one of the greatest track stars in Irish and international athletics.

To put everything in context, in 1954 Roger Bannister became the first person to break the 'unbreakable' four-minute mile. Within two years, Ronnie Delany would match the Englishman's historic achievement, as well as winning an Olympic gold medal in Melbourne.

'In 1954, I had yet to run a mile, and had never been outside Ireland,' he recalls. Two years later, he would become the seventh runner in the world to break the magical four-minute barrier. Six months later, he would be crowned Olympic champion down under, beating the favourite John Landy.

'I was 21 and I felt that I had achieved my destiny.'

A Love of Sport

Ronnie was born on March 6, 1935, just outside Arklow in County Wicklow, but because of his father's work as a Customs and Excise Officer the whole family moved to Dublin and set up home in Sandymount. Living in the south of the city helped Ronnie develop a pure love of all types of sport.

'Once I could lift a racquet or swing a bat, the spontaneous thing was to go out and play sport.'

He spent every free moment playing everything... including tennis and cricket, and running to and from school. 'Unknowingly developing my athleticism and overall body strength,' he points out. The only sport that eluded him was swimming, which he only learned on his honeymoon!

He attended O'Connell CBS on North Richmond Street in Dublin and excelled. The school is named after Daniel O'Connell and has produced scholars, politicians and sportsmen... including an Olympic gold medallist! Ronnie later attended Sandymount High School where he joined the local athletics club, Crusaders AC. Here he was taught the joy of running. At this time, he was not as talented as his brother Joe, but some of the club's mentors encouraged him to hone his talents. In 1952, aged 17, at the Leinster Colleges Championships he was the first Irish schoolboy to break the two-minute barrier at the half mile.

'I didn't know it at the time, but this achievement was to change my life. I immediately began to realise that I had been gifted with a special talent for running. I knew that I wanted to be a great athlete and no one, and no circumstance, could deter me. With dedication that surprised even me, I took control of my own life and made decisions with the foremost goal of furthering my athletics career.'

Ronnie began to win races and understood, 'If you wanted to win... you had to have the utmost desire.'

Traditional Rituals of Prayer

Ronnie has fond memories of attending church as a boy. 'I was a normal boy, saying my prayers that we were taught. The church at this time was quite austere. However, I loved to pray and going to Mass. I made my first communion in Haddington Road Church and that is a treasured memory.' At home, there were traditional rituals of prayer. 'We would have had prayers at meal-time. I also remember the saying of the rosary... and even following the Stations of the Cross!'

For Ronnie, praying remained central to his being. 'Having a personal faith was important to me. It just was a normal thing for young Catholics to pray.' Moving from 'Catholic Ireland' to the United States also meant Ronnie could compare the different expressions of faith, but he was less inclined to warm to

American Catholicism. Ronnie is more of a traditionalist, and still recalls the prayers and music associated with his early youth.

'God is strong and central to my life. He is out there guiding me and giving me lovely things daily. I am not a holy Joe, but I have my personal faith. I like to attend Mass on my terms... attend confession when I wish and receive Holy Communion when appropriate. I also am part of an online prayer group, exchanging little inspiring messages of faith and hope.'

As part of his pre-race preparations, Ronnie would say a prayer.

'Before a race I'd pray on my own.

'I would have my little medal, and some holy water. I would not pray for success, just the ability to run to the best of my ability. I knew that if I ran to the best of my ability, I would win!'

Running to Win

By 1953, he was taking his athletics more seriously and was growing stronger. He took Jack Sweeney's advice of making one decisive move, known as a 'kick', that often carried him to victory when he'd run the half mile. Ronnie possessed lots of natural talent and a good upper body strength, but now he also was clear that if he was to develop further, he would have to train better. He added a new twist to his running... interval training.

Later in 1953, he was accepted as a Cadet in the Irish Army, based in The Curragh, in County Kildare. There were few jobs in Ireland at this period. In Ireland of the 1950s, prospects were bleak and around 500,000 people emigrated during this decade.

But Ronnie quickly realised that he could not combine his new career and running. Much to the dismay of his father, he left the Army. The following year, 1954, he took a job as a salesman based in Co Kilkenny, and he would continue to juggle his new working life and his training regime. 'I just had extraordinary self-belief and an unexplainable instinct that this was where my talents lay,' he stresses. 'This was coupled with an intense dedication to training... and training smart.'

His ambition was to go to America in the footsteps of other Irish runners. He was dreaming big. 'I began to think seriously for the first time about trying for a scholarship. It seemed to make a lot of sense. I could pursue my university education and my athletic career at the one time. It would mean leaving Ireland, but at the time the facilities, coaching and competition in America were the best in the world.'

Living the Dream in Villanova

He applied to attend the famed Augustinian college of Villanova, in Philadelphia, and was accepted on a full scholarship. This decision was crucial on his path towards Melbourne. Ronnie loved America and all aspects of life there. He quickly adapted to a new culture and immersed himself in his sport and academics. He was now running against the best, and developing friendships that would last for the rest of his life.

Quickly enough, the Irishman was christened the 'Villanova Rocket'.

He trained hard and raced for the honour of Ireland and for Villanova. 'I felt I belonged in the dynamic world of American track and field.'

While he did lose a few races, he would go on to run undefeated indoors for five years. The crowds in Boston Garden and Madison Square Garden took him to their hearts! His training and racing regime in 1955 were preparing him for greatness. 'I never lost and I didn't like to lose. In Villanova, the motto was win at all costs. I would do everything possible to win!'

He seldom was not on the podium. When that did happen, 'It made me analyse why I lost... and why I was beaten. Usually, I was tired or injured.' These learnings would help him to go on and turn the tables on his opponents in future races. 'I loved running and racing to win. I also loved to spend time with my fellow runners!'

In 1956, Ronnie was working hard academically in Villanova. On the track, already he was hitting the targets set for selection for the Melbourne Games that November and December. It would not be until October, however, that he would discover he was on the Irish team for Melbourne.

Going for Gold

The Games opened on November 22, with 67 nations represented. 'There is something very special, historic and significant in being sent by your country to an

Olympic Games,' Ronnie reflects. The 1,500 metres preliminary heats would take place a week later. On November 29, Ronnie qualified for the final of the 1,500 metres. Everyone knew that John Landy, the Australian hero, and the second man to break the four-minute mile barrier, was favourite, but it remained an open field. A field that would perform in front of 100,000 fans! Ronnie entered the stadium... 'fancied but not favoured'.

He made his break in the last bend, passed Landy... and won in a time of three minutes and 41.2 seconds.

Gold.

Ronnie did possess an inner belief that he could match anyone. 'I knew if I were to win I would have to make one decisive move. I restrained myself as long as possible and, about 150 yards from the finish, I opened up with everything I had.

'I knew nobody was going to pass me... my legs were pumping like pistons. I was tired but I was not going to give in to anybody. I could hardly believe I had won. My eyes swelled with tears and I dropped to my knees in a prayer of thanksgiving.

'It was a total expression of my faith, recognition of God... and other people, thanking my parents, coaches and everyone who supported me. It was a sense of God's gift to become this one percent of winners in front of the world.

'Going down on my knees was my giving back to the Church!'

He emphasises that on the track, he had to do the running. It wasn't God favouring him! 'There was no God there... just me, I had to bring my intellect. I talked to God before and afterward... but on the track it was Ronnie.'

John Landy came home third and was a gracious loser.

'It was the happiest day of my life. I had set out to win the Olympic 1,500 crown and I had achieved my goal.' Ronnie was aged 21. 'For that day I was grateful to so many people... my parents, my coaches in Ireland... my fellow runners in the U.S.... all who inspired me with confidence and example.'

Lapping the Glory

Ronnie Delaney returned to Ireland and a hero's welcome. He was met by the people of Ireland and welcomed by the Olympic Council and members of government and state.

Ronnie Running Forever

A STATUE HONOURING Ronnie was officially unveiled in his home town of Arklow, located at the roundabout outside Bridgewater Shopping Centre, in November 2021. President Michael D Higgins sent a special message for the occasion, describing Ronnie Delany as a, 'true sporting legend and a wonderful ambassador for Ireland'.

Ronnie was previously honoured by Wicklow County Council with a Civic Reception in 2016, and the naming of an Arklow housing estate after him in 2019. The Cathaoirleach of Arklow Municipal District, Councillor Miriam Murphy, explained, 'We are practically in his front garden as he lived a stone's throw away from this very spot. Only a very small number of athletes have won Olympic medals representing Ireland, and gold medals are particularly scarce, so Ronnie's gold medal at the Melbourne Olympics in 1956 was truly special.'

•••

He returned to college in 1957. He narrowly missed being told to suspend his studies. However, in 1958 he graduated from college. He also had developed an interest in the arts and other college life. 'In my heart I knew I would return to Ireland,' he notes, 'once I had fulfilled my commitments to the track team.'

Recurring injuries led to his retirement from athletics at a young age, in 1962. The *New York Post* wrote, *Nobody has had an indoor mile career to match that of Ronald Michael Delany, who came to Villanova as a 19 year old freshman in 1954. From January 1956-1959 he ran 34 races and won them all.*

'I only wish people in Ireland could have seen me running indoors. The Irish media at the time barely covered my unbeaten career.'

His greatest race, of course, was in Melbourne. He also went to the Rome Olympics in 1960 but made little impact. He knew he was not in the right shape to defend his 1,500 metres crown. He withdrew. 'I ran the Olympics injured and did not do well. Within weeks I would actually beat the medallists... I only lost because of injury,' he says.

'The rest of my athletic career would always be a sort of an anti-climax. I was plagued by injuries later on and I never again had the same driving ambition.'

Winning at such a young age brought with it a new pressure. 'You live with being the Olympic champion every day for the rest of your life. In the short term, if you remain a competitor as I did, it goes with the territory. Every time you step on the starting line you are the target.

'Every athlete wants to beat you, irrespective of the importance of the race. Yours is a scalp to be taken.'

He announced his retirement during the summer of 1962 and got engaged to his fiancée Joan Riordan on the same day.

Olympic Ambassador

Ronnie takes his achievement seriously. 'I wake up every day and I am still an Olympic champion. It impacts on me every day of my life, with people asking me to do things in media and in life.'

Winning gold also means he sees himself as a role model for sport. 'From then on, I was an Olympic champion. To this very day the effect lingers on. There are responsibilities to live up to also. I am always conscious of the need to give youth a good example. I also believe as a champion you should keep in physical shape.'

Ronnie also is grateful and appreciative to point out that if he had not got to Villanova he would not have achieved his dream. 'I think I can answer that question once and for all. There is no doubt in my mind... I would not have won an Olympic title if I had remained in Ireland. I am grateful that I was afforded the opportunity of living in America and attending Villanova. I have reaped a rich harvest for the effort I have put into track and field.'

Ronnie never stopped encouraging young people to take up sport. For this reason, he has always been spoken of fondly. 'I have been greatly honoured by the Irish public and by my peers over the years, and I am so grateful to them.'

Stepping Off the Track

After retiring from competition, he worked in New York for Aer Lingus. After that, for almost 20 years, he was Assistant Chief Executive of B&I Line, based in Dublin and responsible for marketing and operations of the Irish ferry company. In 1998, he established his own firm focused on marketing and sports consultancy.

Since retiring from a work career that also included being part of many state and industry boards, he keeps in touch with fellow Irish Olympian alumni. He is also proud to be president of the Irish Olympian Association and chair of the National Sports Council. He has good relations across all sporting codes, and was part of the founding of *An Gaisce*, the President's Award.

Ronnie Delaney's portrait hangs in the National Gallery of Ireland. He has had stamps issued by *An Post* with his portrait in 1984. In 2006, he was given the Freedom of the City of Dublin. 'I am a Dubliner. My athletic career and life are intrinsically linked to my native city.'

He would now introduce himself as someone who is 'middle-class, educated, has enormous life experience... and has fortuitously enjoyed the success of life, in business and in sport.'

He notes that he does try to be a Christian in all the work that he does with people. He continues to try to make a difference in retirement. 'I help with Friends of the Elderly, and work with Debra Ireland. All these things help me to give something back.'

Reflecting on his life, he acknowledges, 'Looking back on my life and my athletic career, I can have no regrets. I won and lost races. I am grateful for everything I have received in sport and out of sport.'

He has great memories to cherish. 'I still have my miraculous medal and holy water from when I raced.'

He has no regrets and would like his epitaph to be something factual, perhaps… 'Olympic Champion, Gold Medal Winner, December 1, 1956'.

●●●

'My Granny turned to God for strength. I take this as an important life lesson, for me too to be able to turn to God for strength. However, when I run... it is all me.'

ciara mageean

ATHLETE

CIARA MAGEEAN IS from the generation that grew up in the years post 'the Troubles' and enjoyed a life which benefited from the peace process in Northern Ireland. Ciara is from Portaferry, in Down, a small town near Strangford Lough. She grew up in a Catholic-majority area. Camogie and Irish dancing were two of her twin loves as a child, true traditional Irish endeavours.

She attended the local St Mary's primary school, and while camogie and Irish dancing were closest to her heart, Ciara took part in anything that was happening in the locality. Tap dancing and drama were also on her 'to do' list. She went to secondary school in Ballynahinch, where her mother had attended also. It was only when she got the opportunity to take up running in secondary school, that she found her... magical place. 'That's where I started getting into athletics,' she notes. 'My PE teacher spotted that I never stopped running around.'

That observant teacher encouraged her to take up cross-country running. 'I was repeatedly told by the PE class teacher that… "PE is not the Olympics!"' The Olympic Games would have to wait a little longer… In 2016, Ciara became the Irish indoor 1,500 metres record holder and qualified to represent her country at the Rio Games!

Whilst in secondary school, her running opportunities really took off. Aged around 14, a teacher suggested that she try track running. 'I jumped at this. This is where I found my true calling. My track running was better than cross country.'

Gradually, she was gaining a reputation and was invited to be part of the Northern Ireland talent academy. This would lead her to going to University College Dublin on a scholarship to continue her education, and where she was also able to seriously focus on her running.

As a teenager, Ciara regularly broke Sonia O'Sullivan's underage records. Gradually she was wining and representing Ireland at international meetings. In 2009 she won a silver medal at the World Youth Championships, and repeated this performance at the World Junior Championships the following year. Her first senior international competition resulted in a 10th place finish in the 1,500 metres at the 2010 Commonwealth Games in Delhi, where she was representing Northern Ireland.

She set her sights on making the 2012 Olympics but was knocked off course by the first of a series of debilitating injuries. Surgery on a bone spur in her ankle allowed her to make a comeback in 2014 when she won the Irish 1,500 metres title… but disaster struck again. She missed most of the 2015 season, including the European Indoor Championships, through an injury to her other foot.

At this time, she combined her studies in physiotherapy, and balanced student life with that of an elite athlete. She was also lucky at this time to come under the guidance of Jerry Kiernan.

She credits Kiernan for so much of what she has achieved in her running career. A former Olympian, and marathon champion, Kiernan was perhaps best known for being an athletics media pundit on RTE.

'Jerry began coaching me prior to my ankle surgery. He took me on while I was possibly in the worst place I have ever been as an athlete. Jerry helped coach and guide me through not only the physical training back from my surgery, but he also proved to be a great friend.

'He was there through my tears and my triumphs.'

Her deeper crisis was… who she was, if she was not running? Here, Kiernan offered Ciara a 'life lesson' in understanding that her identity and her whole being was greater than just being a 'runner'. That discovery, and full understanding, allowed her to see beyond the lows of being an injured athlete. Jerry Kiernan, Ciara's mentor and coach, died in January 2021.

Injury free in 2016, Ciara claimed bronze in the 1,500 metres at the European

Championships. The following year, she was fortunate in moving to Manchester where she joined a professional running team – Team New Balance – one of the few in Europe. She now had a rhythm of races to focus on within the four-year Olympic cycle.

'I am lucky to be a professional athlete,' Ciara confesses. 'I am blessed to have the talent and the ability to do something with this gift.'

Family Matters

While she acknowledges many teachers and coaches as key influences, it is clear Ciara's family played a key role in her life. Their competitiveness and achievements helped her sharpen her own ambition. Her father Christopher was a midfielder on the Down hurling team, and was nicknamed 'The Hunter' for his ability to chase the ball all day long. Her mother Catherine was a camogie player. Her older sister Máire, now a doctor, won a camogie Ulster Colleges All Star in 2008. Two years later, Ciara did likewise for her school, Assumption Grammar in Ballynahinch.

She acknowledges, in particular, her mother and also credits her granny as being a huge influence in her life. Growing up in a Catholic family she has memories of prayer at home all through her childhood.

She recalls her mother praying with her, and singing her and her siblings to sleep! Before school, her granny would occasionally bring all the children to morning Mass in their local parish which was beside her school. Many other families were there too. It was a normal part of her growing up to be at church and play sport.

'I still go to Mass when I am at home,' she explains. 'I also went during my college years. However this is a challenge now as my Sunday-long run takes priority over others things (including Mass), however even here in Manchester I am still drawn to going to Mass in a local church. I try to go as often as I can.'

Like other athletes she does acknowledge the current struggle of practicing her faith and training. For her, her faith offers peace. Attending Mass for her is about connecting with her upbringing, knowing that at home her family are doing the same. Her faith is about finding peace, purpose and contentment. It connects her to who she is and where she came from.

'This is something I think about when I travel. On international trips, no

It's Good to Talk

L IKE EVERY ELITE athlete, Ciara knows that everything can 'disappear' with one muscle tear. Years of work can be left... in dust. 'It's something I constantly work on, trying to stay resilient,' she explained. 'To be honest, a lot of it is conversation. It's accepting that it's okay to be disappointed in that moment.

'I kind of view it as a bereavement cycle... mourning the loss of something. Now, that obviously sounds dramatic. It's obviously not the same as losing someone. But in that moment, I'm mourning the loss of an opportunity to go and race, something that I spend lots of time preparing for and you kind of have to allow yourself to go through those emotions.

'You don't beat yourself up. But you should recognise the emotion you are feeling. If you recognise that you're staying there for too long, then maybe that's the time you reach out for help. I'm lucky I have a great sports psychologist and I chat to her.'

•••

matter where I am, I often try to get to the local chapel. It became a running joke… I would go to the management and ask about Mass nearby? I know other senior runners would ask too, and go as a group. In Rio at the games, a few of us tried to find a wee chapel.

'An interesting memory is, we ended up in a church that wasn't Catholic… but it was similar.'

On another occasion, in Montreal, Ciara's desire to get to Mass resulted in many of the team going with her. She is happy to talk to her friends about her faith in quiet moments, but a 'private' conversation is something she prefers rather than talking publicly.

Prayer remains a part of Ciara's life. While she might not turn to God in times of challenge in her running preparations, she is very much still aware of her need to be spiritually connected.

'My spiritual side is also important, and I get healing from that too.'

She still tries to stay connected to her family traditions. Her mother remains an important religious figure in her life, and Ciara recalls her mother sending her a book, *Dipping into Lent*. 'I try to observe Lent, as do many of my fellow athletes.' Her mother has also sent her a statue of Our Lady. Her family have a tradition of having a family May altar, which used to be common in Ireland.

'I travel with a set of rosary beads. I don't use them all the time, but they can help me pray, sleep… and focus. They also help me to connect with… and remind me of my granny and her prayer life.'

'Granny loved the rosary and had all the cousins praying in May in her house… the house was full of rosary beads. This was normal for us growing up.'

She also recalls another time visiting her Granny, 'When she ended up in hospital, I visited her and I waited outside her booth as she was praying. She had a devotion to the Sacred Heart of Jesus and often recited… *Sacred Heart of Jesus, I place all my trust in you.*

'My Granny turned to God for strength. I take this as an important life lesson, for me too to be able to turn to God for strength. However, when I run… it is all me.'

'Around racing, I am not tapped into the emotional side of me. I focus on the racing only. I do have a small vessel of holy water, and I might bless myself leaving the house. However, I don't pray to win… only just to get through the next challenge. It is not for God to intervene, just to give me the strength to cope with whatever happens.' For Ciara her faith is something personal and she is not into public expressions like other sports people on the international stage.

Dealing with Success

Ciara had her moments of questioning through injury and disappointments. She experienced, in total, a period of three years where she was unable to run. 'I didn't have an Irish vest for this time. I was worried what people would think... that perhaps I was just a good junior and not ready for senior running.'

While she wants to win, Ciara is very focused on what is coming next. She believes in herself, but knows that her success is all about talent *and* hard work. Her self-determination is what got her to this stage in her life. She may not pray or thank God for success, but takes delight in sharing her success with her family back in the parish of Portaferry.

'I don't thank God for my gifts.

'I have worked hard for my success. Yet I do remember a priest praying for me before a race. I liked that. Like others, I have my struggles with my faith, but I appreciate little gestures of prayer... the lighting of the candles.

'We can all turn to prayer and do good acts for others... this is not something exclusive to people of faith. It's complicated! I am grateful for the strength from God; but I don't thank God for my success.'

Her simplicity of a faith rooted in family is admirable. This faith is grounded in the Catholic tradition, and her prayer and spiritual life are embedded in that too. While she still has many questions about her faith, she is very much aware of God being present in her life.

'I can recognise the various influences of all the people who brought me to where I am today... my family, teachers and trainers. Maybe the hand of God was working through all these people. I get meaning from all these people and especially my family.'

Ciara Mageean would like to be remembered for, 'being kind, thoughtful and all those qualities in life I hold dear. My values in life and my passion are not all in sport. I believe I was put here on earth to help others!'

Ciara is not finished yet. She has plans for many more races. She participated at the Tokyo Olympics in 2021, and had an outstanding 2022 season, winning silver medals at both the Commonwealth Games and also the European Championships.

However, ever since her mentor Jerry Kiernan instilled the value that there is more to Ciara than 'just a runner', she knows there is a long life ahead off the track.

●●●

'My mother had a strong Catholic faith and she worked on the principle that if you wanted your dinner or lunch, then you went to Mass. I have no recollection of family prayer at home. Our faith was private and personal.'

earl mccarthy

SWIMMER

EARL McCARTHY FOUND it easy to start swimming. Unlike most Irish children, there was a pool available to him because of his father's work. However, to be the best he could be, and to become an Olympian, Earl had to pack his bags and head abroad. There was no more Ireland could do for him.

After retiring from his sport and then making a comeback by heading to Europe, Earl realised his dream, and competing in the freestyle at the Atlanta Olympics in 1996.

Growing up in Dublin's northside, in the Donnycarney area, Earl, who is now swim coach in UCD, recalls that his mother just wanted her children to learn to swim as a basic life skill.

'I started to swim in Raheny, in a pool that is now gone. My sister and I were part of the club. She gave up around the age of 10, but I continued… I was showing promising results. That is simply how I got started.'

There was no plan to focus on swimming. Sport was in his family, and his dad had an amateur background in cycling, but his dad was also happy for his son to follow a different sporting pursuit.

Swimming it was, then!

'Swimming is very solitary,' he explains. 'You can have good friends around you. However, when you push off… you are on your own, and with your own thoughts. I have reflected on this and there is something meditative for the swimmer repeating actions and rhythms.

'Unlike team sports, the swimmer might be in a pool with other people, but you are left to your own thoughts. Even at the early morning sessions, I remember no one wanted to talk! The culture was about being quiet.

'Just do your thing with little or no conversation.

'It doesn't matter if it's a 25 metres or a 50 metres pool... swimming is very repetitious. The only thing you hear is the water!

'For me, the resilience I got from swimming was the belief that I was good at it. I believed I could further improve. In my early teens I was doing really well. It was all about hard work and fine tuning your talent.' He adds, 'There were other swimmers who were not as good. However, I used to wonder what motivated them to get out of bed to swim at 5.30am in the morning. And swimmers are in the pool twice a day... unlike other team sports, where there might be only a couple of training sessions and a match each week.

'Swimming was 30 years ahead of most other sports when it came to intense training.

'Swimmers had a different life, and I was conscious that my life was different to that of my friends at school. I finally gave up swimming at around 18. I did a few courses and took a job as a porter in a hospital.

'The reason I gave up was that I stopped winning around the ages of 16 to 18. The transition from junior to senior was very hard.'

A Dinner for a Mass

'I would call myself a Christian. Growing up we all had to go to Mass as a family. My mother had a strong Catholic faith and she worked on the principle that if you wanted your dinner or lunch, then you went to Mass. I have no recollection of family prayer at home. Our faith was private and personal.'

Earl notes that the family ethos was that you needed some type of religious framework rather than nothing. These values have a strong resonance for him to have some type of faith, regardless of the tradition.

'I believe in that form of spirituality where meditation and visualisation can help focus and assist an athlete prepare before competition. Instead of abstract goals, build up an image of where you want to be.

'You have to believe in the potential.'

Even after packing in the sport as a young adult, Earl had that nagging feeling that he had more to achieve in swimming, however. His dream was to qualify to swim at the Olympics. 'I couldn't just get over the fact that I hadn't qualified for the Olympics in 1988. I couldn't let it go.'

Around this time his results were still not as good as he would have liked. 'You eat a lot of humble pie! When you see other people qualify... and I am missing out!? So I just gave up.' He needed a change or environment.

'I moved to Germany. I wanted to make a comeback.

'Swimming in Ireland back then was terrible... poor resources for anyone seeking success. This is a reality for speciality niche sports, if you want to succeed, just like in cycling, you need to leave and go somewhere else to improve. Even today, the reality is the same for young athletes in many sports... the resources are just not there.'

'On my comeback, I just missed out qualifying for the 1992 Olympics in Barcelona after months of intensive training. Then I made my decision... I was going to follow a path taken by some of Ireland's greatest cyclists, the likes of Sean Kelly, Stephen Roache... Shay Elliot... I was going to Europe.

'At first I moved to Hamburg for a few weeks... and eventually stayed for 10 years. I trained at an elite performance centre. Things began to improve for me from there.'

'You have to be in the right environment. I just couldn't let it go. All my teenage life was focused on going to the Olympics.' He notes that other people he knew just gave up, even though they might have been better than him. Earl was determined and focused.

'I was 27 when I went to the Olympics. It was like I was possessed with this dream...

Mental, Emotional, Spiritual

'I believe Irish athletes don't make it because they are Irish, but in spite of the fact that they are Irish. Just look at our cyclist and swimmers. These are internationally more popular sports. However, in Ireland, sport is dominated by the GAA,

Believing

EARL MCCARTHY HAD turned his back on swimming at 19 years of age, but he found his way back to the pool. He qualified for the Olympic Games in 1996, and in 2003 he became the oldest male winner of an Irish Championship when he won the 100 metres freestyle. Earl was 33 years old... and still believing.

•••

and rugby and soccer, and team sports. Against the odds, as a country we have managed to produce champions in cycling and swimming.

'You need to be determined. You have to make it on mental, emotional and spiritual platforms.'

It was not easy trying to improve at his sport. 'Even while living in Hamburg. I had to take on extra jobs just to cover my swimming expenses… my dreams. My days were long combining paying jobs and training.'

He acknowledges that his best years were from 1994 to '96. A big breakthrough for Earl was his performance to qualify for the European Championships in 1995. 'I began to get good results around this time. If I can compete with the Germans, then I knew I was on the right path.'

'Of course I could win in Ireland, but to win against the elite was important in order to advance in the sport.' He competed for Ireland at the 1996 Olympics in Atlanta, in a swim team that included four other members, Michelle Smith, Marion Madine, Nick O'Hare and Adrian O'Connor. In the 100 metres Earl finished seventh in round one in a time of 50.99, and fourth in round one in the 200 metres freestyle with a time of 1.53.67 (Earl was the Irish record holder and national champion in both events).

Giving Back

'I hit a wall after the Olympics. I walked away.

'It was years before I got back into a pool. I was done. I didn't miss it at all.'

As he was approaching his thirtieth birthday, however, a chance conversation with a friend, who was an officer in the army, left Earl dwelling on a proposal.

'I had lived in Germany for 10 years. I was asked if I would like to help in Galway with some swimmers there. Initially, I committed to doing this for a few months. Galway felt like a good place to live after my time in Germany.'

Soon he was hooked again, and surrounded by swimmers with great potential.

Earl acknowledged that his friend knew that once he started to coach young people that contact would lead him to stay for longer. 'I was supposed to go for a few weeks… and ended up staying for five years!'

'I left Galway in 2005 for another coaching role in Dublin. Initially, this was to be for a year.' This was the beginning of a new chapter in Earl's life. Having left school early, he also returned to education. 'I noticed that many of the young people I was coaching were in college. I had the same daily rhythm as them. They trained... went to college and trained.' He realised he could return to education too. At first, he studied Sports Management.

'I got the bug for education. This led to post-grad courses and qualifying with a law degree and finally a Doctorate.'

This path led to an unexpected invitation to be part of a new pool complex being built in UCD. Taking on the role meant Earl deciding to pause his training to be a barrister in favour of a new role in coaching future Ireland swimmers.

Swimming became central in his life once more.

He was appointed as *Women In Sport* manager for Swim Ireland in 2008, and became a swimming analyst for RTE.

'There is an injustice for some sports people in Ireland,' he explains.

'It is a very male-orientated world, and it was tougher for women to be involved. A lack of respect and acknowledgement for minority sports also existed. I am still driven to fight for people, to help them strive for a chance of success within sport, but with a safety net of an education on the basis that it might not work out.

'Too many people in sport just never got the opportunity to shine, and neither did they have a back-up plan.'

A Life Path

Earl admits that there was a path in his life that he was meant to be on. 'As I get older, I see how I have been guided along in my life. As I look back, I can see the people who helped me... my parents, coaches... many good people. As an arrogant determined teenager, I didn't see that.

'What I achieved in sport was all through hard work. Maybe a potential was within me as a gift... and I just brought it to the fore through this hard work.

'Is it God given, yes.

'Your job as an athlete is to reveal it. Everyone is given it in different measures. It is our job to find this revelation... it's a duty for yourself, in whatever sport you give your life to.'

Earl recalls the words of The Beatles manager, Brian Epstein... 'Fill in the gaps that God left out'. As a sports director, he must now help fill in the gaps for a new generation of swimmers.

He notes a few lines from his dad's eulogy... from John 2:17... *Great things I have done, even greater things you will do.* 'These are the words of a coach and a leader.

'They are my words now.'

●●●

'In the extreme endurance sports, it is so hard... if you don't have a belief beyond yourself maybe it can be harder to get results. You need to dig deep. If you are in the zone, it is almost like an experience of prayer.'

gladys ganiel

ATHLETE

GLADYS GANIEL IS an example to us all, to never stop!

Born in Maine, in the United States, she always ran. At collegiate level she excelled at Providence in the mid- to late-90s, and was a member of the NCAA Championship cross-country team. She came to Ireland to live in 1999.

In 2014, she competed for Northern Ireland at the Commonwealth Games in Glasgow, recording her second fastest time ever in the marathon and finishing 12th in a time of 2.40.29. Three years later, at 40 years of age, she ran her fastest time ever … 2.37.55 in Berlin. The next year she helped Team Ireland to eighth place at the European Championships in Berlin. In 2019, in Dublin, she ran faster still… 2.36.42.

Gladys was 42 years old and was not stopping. In May 2022, she won the Belfast City Marathon.

Maine offered a healthy lifestyle, and lots of sport, for young boys and girls. In high school, basketball was the number one attraction for Gladys. 'I started running to get in shape for basketball. My neighbours were into cross-country running, so I watched them and thought that was something I could do to get fit for basketball.' She was 12 years of age, and quickly discovered that not only was she a good basketball player, but had a perfect endurance for running.

After high school, she obtained an athletic scholarship for Providence. There,

Gladys first encountered the famous Irish trainer Ray Treacy, who was head coach. His brother John, the Olympic silver medallist in the Los Angeles marathon, also went to this college. (Ray Treacy remains head coach in Providence where a new track has been named after him)

In her four years at Providence, Gladys was surrounded by many Irish runners, and in 1995 the college won an NCAA Division I National Championship cross country. Gladys remembers joking with others that she was a 'token American' on the team!

A Question of Salvation

Gladys is originally from a small town called Harrington, on the northern coast of Maine, a small fishing village which also offered work on surrounding large-scale blueberry farms. Some of her family still live there, where the religious culture is evangelical. This is a more northern style and different from Southern Baptist expressions of faith. It is conversative in its values and traditions.

She notes that her experience of church attendance is positive. Her church was more low church, with a Puritan tradition. This was normal in that area of Maine. 'It was a positive influence on my life,' she affirms. An important part of this tradition was the question of salvation and making the decision to take Jesus into your life.

In her own words, 'To be saved and to take Jesus into your life was important…a conversion experience was key to being part of the church. I had a conversion experience at the age of seven. I wrote the date into my King James Bible. I received Christ as my saviour into my life.

'This took place with the wife of the pastor at the First Baptist Church of Harrington! This was a real public profession of faith.'

God was important to Gladys, and has continued to be so. The strong puritan culture was important to her and she carried these forward in her life. 'Also, what was instilled… was that you have a great responsibility… those who have been given a gift have a responsibility to do something with it.

'If you have a gift, you have a responsibility to do something with it, or disappoint God!' That work ethic is embedded in her culture and ultimately her sport. This has also been ingrained in her personality.

However, her family was not really into sport, and Gladys was the only one who took sport seriously! Her sisters and mother played some sport, and her dad grew up Catholic in New Jersey before he joined the navy and he kept fit through his physical work as a builder.

High Performance Environment equals Pressure

In college, she applied herself to her new routine. Whilst she was on a scholarship programme, she was also aware that running was a part-time job. In Providence, she had access to various running opportunities. 'We had indoor, outdoor and cross country. You had to train hard and work hard at your education. Ray Treacy was a great teacher and coach.' Being in a High-Performance environment brought with it... high pressure.

She had a natural love for running and never viewed it as a sacrifice. Gladys says it was her choice to run. It was a passion and something she could enjoy.

When she first came to Ireland in 1999, she found the country to be very secular and not as religious as she had read about. 'Around 2000 Ireland seemed to be a secular place... more than I expected. At the same time, I was studying religion. Yet I did meet some who had found that faith was important to them.' She attended Grosvenor Road Baptist Church in Dublin, which at that time had many young people and had a vibrant community, which she enjoyed.

'Around the time of my MA and PhD I didn't run much, I was focused on my studies. I did some running with a local club in Dundrum South Dublin.'

After her Providence years Gladys won the NCAA's Walter Byers Award for the top student-athlete in the United States, which funded her graduate study overseas. She studied in University College Dublin for an MA in Politics 2001, and subsequently a doctorate (2005). Her PhD was on evangelicalism, conflict and reconciliation in Northern Ireland.

She had some personal pressure to complete her studies, as she had a three-year scholarship from the Royal Irish Academy and needed to complete within this time frame.

In 2006, after her doctorate in 2005 she got her first job with the Irish School of Ecumenics in Belfast, which is part of Trinity College. She held this position

In the Mind

GLADYS HAS WRITTEN on her website 'Building a Church without Walls' about her preparation for the marathon, and her mind.

'I try not to think about it. Dwelling on your opponents or how you will cope with the sheer agony of running 26.2 miles as fast as you can may not damage your legs or your lungs, but it will drain your brainpower,' she has written.

'Eliud Kipchoge, the first man to run under two hours for a marathon, put it this way, "It is better for the body to be tired, than the mind".'

When Gladys takes her place on the starting line of a marathon, she does not think about the finish.

'Former marathon world record holder Paula Radcliffe kept herself in the moment by counting from 1 to 100, over and over. I have my own secret mantra to repeat. If you get this right in a race – and I don't always do – when you are finished it seems like the marathon has passed in the twinkling of an eye.

'But marathon running has taught me that fantasising about the finish won't make it come any sooner.'

●●●

for the next nine years lecturing on conflict resolution. After marriage and settling down, she then reconnected with her passion and love for running.

She recalls, 'From my youth, I was always told I would eventually be a long distance runner. Once I got settled in Belfast, I trained seriously to get to the level of being able to run the Olympic qualifying mark for the marathon.'

By this time, Gladys had received Irish citizenship. She has represented Ireland at two European championships – 2016 half marathon, 2018 marathon. Because of her residency in Northern Ireland, she qualified for the Commonwealth Games marathon in 2014, finishing 12th.

Human Potential

'When you are young, you think God will help you, but as I got older it was less about winning, and more about doing something with the ability I was given... and give an honest effort with that talent. This almost was my prayer. Empirically God can't make everyone win! It is more about realising your own human potential.

'If you have a gift, you have a duty to do your best with it.' Her Maine upbringing still had a big influence on her outlook on life.

She also found that some runners from Africa are quite devout in their personal expression of faith, but Gladys is comfortable with different forms of expression. Attending Providence helped her feel comfortable among different faith traditions. She has admired Meb Keflezighi from Eritrean, who came to the US as a refugee and won the Olympic silver medal in the marathon... representing his adopted country in Athens.

'He is an understated person. An amazing runner and orthodox Christian with a strong, quiet faith. He is not brash about his faith, like some American sportspeople, but rather takes the approach that he is developing the gifts God has given him to the best of his ability.'

Gladys does concede though that having a faith and being active in sport at times might overlap. Reflecting on this type of faith in God she notes, 'In the extreme endurance sports, it is so hard... if you don't have a belief beyond yourself maybe it can be harder to get results. You need to dig deep. If you are in the zone, it is almost like an experience of prayer.

'Time almost stands still. You are eternally present…like an experience of prayer. Psychologists might call it something else, but I'd call it prayer.'

Knocking at the Door

Looking to the future, Gladys still feels she can keep running for another few years, as she is still in her early 40s. Her personal times are still in a zone where she feels she is knocking at the door with qualifying for other championships.

She has a little regret that she might have performed better during her college years, wondering if she spent too much time studying… and might have trained harder if she hadn't studied so hard. However, she enjoyed studying and believes God had a plan for her beyond running.

'She also has a passion for her work in Queen's lecturing in sociology. She sees this career as a vocation, educating the next generation, who can go on to make a difference in making Northern Ireland society a better place (or, for the international students, taking what they learn in Northern Ireland back home.) Much of her research is concerned with understanding the role of churches in peace-building and contributing to social justice, and she hopes lessons from her research can have a wider societal impact.

Gladys just wants to be remembered for who she is… someone who has never stopped.

●●●

'The spirit, the will to win, and the will to excel are the things that endure. These qualities are so much more important than the events that occur.'

— Vince Lombardi

American Football Coach
(1913-1970)

'I haven't really thought if God was guiding me. I have believed that God has had a plan for me. I just haven't really got the correct answer yet... maybe I am too young!'

deirbhile o'keeffe

TENNIS PLAYER

DEIRBHILE O'KEEFFE HAS has a twin sister Seona, and that made her lucky to begin with in life. 'Having a doubles partner who understands you is important,' she explains. 'Also Seona is left handed… and I am right handed, a perfect combination.

'Having a twin meant I always had someone to play against.'

As a sportsperson, she considers herself very competitive. 'I am very competitive, sports-mad and a hard-working individual. That's how it has been since my childhood.'

Deirbhile, from Raheny, is now a PE and science teacher in Loreto Secondary School in Dalkey, has been playing tennis since her childhood. Many young people take part in sport and have dreams of making the break into the higher elite level, but most have to ultimately make a decision around their future, and need to balance their love to compete with forging a working career away from the sporting arena.

Deirbhile is representative of many young people who reach that crossroads.

Twin Goals

Having a twin growing up meant that Deirbhile and Seona often decided to separate at different times in school, sometimes choosing different study classes in order to remain apart. However, in their teens they became closer. Deirbhile notes that it was important for both to develop separately and have independent friendships.

'From the age of 16, we became closer again.' Sport was a big part of the O'Keeffe household, with the girls' dad running marathons and their mum playing tennis. 'Sport was always there at home.'

But which to choose? For Deirbhile tennis brought a lot of positive experiences, and not just in winning tournaments. Taking part in competition was extra special in itself, and it kept Deirbhile and Seona active and busy. Deirbhile also had friends who were not much into sport. 'Having friends who were different and not really playing sport was very important to me.'

She found being able to navigate these relationships, and maintain her passion for sport, a balancing act. It helped to have good people to guide her. Her parents were crucial in her tennis journey, but Deirbhile also had the influence of her tennis coach Alan Beaddie. 'While I was beginning to play and enter competitions his influence was great… almost a father figure.' She also thanks her PE teacher, Niamh Ward who also was a positive guiding influence.

Generation to Generation

'I was close to my granny in Moyglass, in Tipperary, and remember that on visits to her we would say the rosary every night. For me, my early religious memories are positive and joy-filled and related to family.'

'Our family was close, and I learned a lot about faith from them. It just was a normal part of growing up… having a faith passed on from generation to generation.

'Between the ages of 11 to 14 I did not have a lot of self-belief. I was training to play. I never really knew the difference between training to play and training to win. It took me a while to understand how I could train to win… rather than just match practice.

'Having self-belief is important in sport and it took me a while to understand this fine line.'

Deirbhile also took a further step in self-belief when, in 2019, she took part in World Youth Day, an International Catholic event for young people. 'I attended and was completely out of my comfort zone. I was at an international faith event, far from home, with other young Catholics. But the event had a big impact on me, and because of how I was received by the people in Panama, I understand the importance of being welcoming and hospitable to different people from other countries… and denominations and faith.

'I have brought this into my teaching in the classroom. I also had the privilege of carrying the Irish flag at the opening ceremony in Panama City with Pope Francis.'

Before competing in a tennis event, Deirbhile looks to her grandad for help. 'I might not necessarily pray to God, but I would try to connect with my grandad, who died when I was very young. I ask for his guidance, whether I'm winning or losing. He is my Guardian Angel!

'My family always told me grandad would be looking down on me.'

There were other moments of prayer in her life, however. 'I would say a prayer before I travelled to play. I even say a prayer before a job interview, but it is more a conversation rather than a structured prayer.'

Character and Confidence

With a combination of good coaching and increased determination as a 15- and 16-year-old, Deirbhile learned how to achieve small incremental points in order to gain an edge over an opponent. 'Being able to gain points… to gain a set and to win a match, is dependent upon a mindset that all tennis players work on. I began to realise I was doing really good training sessions which led me to win.

'Small steps resulted in me getting access to playing at a higher level and ranking. I could see the benefits. Winning gave me confidence, but my coaches were crucial at that stage of my development. They gave me belief as a teenager, instilling the value of what it takes to win… and where winning brings you.'

Character building, motivation and confidence are such important parts that many sports people acquire on their journey through their careers. Deirbhile was not just training smart, but was also delving into many sports books, looking for a psychological sharpness and greater focus during play. It helped too to watch a lot of tennis on television and feast on reruns of old matches.

Twin Goals

DEIRBHILE AND SEONA, like the Williams sisters on the World stage, had to look deep into one another's eyes and souls as tennis players. Except, Venus and Serena Williams, when they met in the US Open final in 2001... weren't twins!

When in Clontarf Tennis Club they both entered two events in the Leopardstown Junior Open, the under-16s and under-18s Singles. And they both won through to face each other in both finals.

The girls were offered the option to play just one final with a winner takes all result. However, they both insisted they would play two finals against each other on the same day.

Deirbhile O'Keeffe was crowned under-16 champion, and then the tables were reversed when Seona won the under-18 final.

●●●

'Doing everything that it takes to win also involves having a positive attitude, even when things are not going your way,' she notes. 'All of this makes you want to win more.'

Deirbhile liked to dream big, like every kid and young adult.

'My dream was to travel and make a career out of tennis. I attended so many tournaments as a spectator. From an early age, my dream was to be involved in sport… and I knew tennis was my path. I could visualise myself playing in some of the amazing tournaments.'

Ireland's Women's Fed Cup team was her goal.

Deirbhile did not make the team, but has no regrets. 'It sounds weird based on what I have said so far, but at this stage of my life I was a happy teenager, transitioning from school to college and playing competitive sport. In order to commit to that team, I would have had to go to the US to college, to focus only on tennis.

'By choosing to stay in Ireland, I was able to focus on my career. I really did want to be a teacher… so I had a sporting dream, but also I had a career dream too. It was a choice I had to make.'

So many of her competitors were taking the path towards scholarships, and some of Deirbhile's friends are now on the tennis circuit in the US and seeking to forge a full-time career in their sport. Deirbhile made a tough decision, but one which spoke to her from her heart.

'I realised I wanted to play tennis as a lifestyle sport more than a career.

'I remain really ambitious, and have learned how to do whatever it takes to win. I admire people in sport… like Novak Djokovic, who are very public about their faith. That strength of character impresses me.' But Deirbhile believes she did not make any huge sacrifice in deciding not to put her sport first and centre in her adult life.

'In my youth, I sacrificed a lot and missed out on a social life, like other girls. I didn't drink alcohol as I was minding my body as a teenager. I committed fully to training in my teens… I was strict with everything.

'I was determined to lead a regimental lifestyle, in order to be the best that I could be. I also sacrificed playing other sports because I chose tennis first. Saying no to friends was tough, but I had to believe in myself and not doubt the decisions and sacrifices I was making. It has to come from within you.'

New Choices

'I am now in a time of my life where I can make new choices. At one time I played only tennis, which is an individual sport... and it is all on you. I have never played team sports. I now want to play a new team sport and get good at it quickly. That's what attracted me to Tag Rugby. I bring speed and strength to the team. I absolutely love it... I'm almost addicted to it!'

She is happy with her new sporting ambition, and confident her past experiences in tennis will help her. 'As a PE teacher, I want to have skills in a number of sports. I want to learn how to play at a high level in as many sports as I can.'

There remain few regrets. 'Maybe I should have gone to America for the scholarship. However, to be honest, what I got out of my choice to stay in Ireland resulted in me being able to travel... and spend three summers in the States working as a tennis coach.

'I am thankful for everything I have done in my sporting life. For me, it has given me character... and knowing what I can do. I would not have this if I did not play tennis.'

Deirbhile is involved with a leadership programme with Tennis Ireland, focusing on Women in Sport. 'I am passionate about this... it is massive to get girls to make friends within tennis, so that they will all stay in touch with sport. Peer support is important for young girls.'

She has had great mentors, people who have guided her at important places in her life. Does that include God?. 'I haven't really thought if God was guiding me. I have believed that God has had a plan for me. I just haven't really got the correct answer yet... maybe I am too young!

'But I do see a meaning in everything I have done. It is good to have moments of reflection, where I try to figure out where I have been... and maybe where I am going!'

Deirbhile would like to be remembered as someone who has made a difference in the lives of others. 'Inspiring one young person, and to make a difference in even one life,' that she believes, is what we are all here to do.

●●●

'Before a big event, I usually go to church and light a candle for St Sebastian, who is the patron saint of athletes.'

– Simone Biles

Gymnast and Olympic Medallist

'Happiness does not live in
fame or fortune. When we are
content or happy, that is when
we are close to our source.'

catherina mckiernan

ATHLETE

CATHERINA MCKIERNAN, FROM a young age, loved freedom and confidence that running gave her, and throughout her brilliant career she raced like a woman... happy and free.

By the end of her competitive career in 2004, Catherina was rightly heralded as one of the world's greatest cross-country runners.

She conquered Ireland first, but gold eluded her on the greatest stage of all. But there were no regrets... how could there be!

An Olympian, Catherina was not just a four-time World cross-country silver medallist, but was the best in Europe, and also won the London, Berlin and Amsterdam marathons. She still reigns as the Irish marathon record holder.

From the parish of Cornafean, in Cavan, she grew up on a farm as the youngest of seven 'From a young age, I loved the feeling... I just ran around the fields at home. I don't really know why I went out to be honest... I suppose it was just that feeling of well-being.'

She fondly recalls winter evenings, when it was too dark and wet to go outside, that she would just run on the spot for 40 minutes or so. She was a talented camogie player too, and to begin with, she had absolutely no ambition to run races in her early teens. 'It wasn't something I had dreamt about.

'I just did it because I loved running.'

Cycle or Run

Running is not synonymous with Cavan. It was a county renowned for team sports and one which has a rich GAA heritage, synonymous with winning football teams in the middle of the late century, including in an epic All-Ireland final against Kerry played in New York's Polo Grounds.

Catherina fondly thinks of her upbringing. 'Cornafean is very rural. I was very active from an early age, but I had no ambition to compete. For girls… they played camogie… and boys football. These were the only options!' she says. When she was 14, Catherina won an Intermediate Camogie Championship medal.

'In school I played camogie and I loved it, as it was a team sport. I also played a bit of badminton… not to mention playing football in the fields with my brothers. Back in these days, if you needed to go anywhere you had to cycle or run! I was just very fit from daily activity.'

Catherina had attended Loreto in Cavan, and only in her last year was an athletic club established. With very little training, she won the All-Ireland schools title.

As she stresses, 'there wasn't a lot of running then. It was all steps. It was all a gradual progression. When I won the All-Ireland schools, that was my first big day.

'It was simple. I was running in my bare feet.'

Cross-Country

Catherina started running with Cornafean. It was clear she had a talent, and soon she came to the attention of Joe Doonan, who was a local teacher. He was also a well-known coach who would nurture and guide Catherina to success.

In her first year of structured training, she started to accumulate wins in various cross-country races and titles. 'I got a coach, a family friend, who felt it would be good to pursue my talent more. This was Fr Oliver O'Reilly. He contacted my coach Joe Doonan. That's where it all started. Success came quickly… winning senior Ireland titles.

'I then ran in some European races and picked up wins too.

'Joe was an amazing mentor… he planned my training, my races, my schedule.

We worked well together. I didn't say much and he liked that. I always did a bit extra too. If I had not found competition running, I would have still found the love of running. I like being active and the feeling of well-being.

'I didn't start running until 1988, and by '92 I had a World silver medal!' The progress was fairly quick.' Catherina had just turned 22.

After school, Catherina had devoted herself to training. She also took a job with the local county council. Rather than follow other Irish athletes, who relocated abroad, Catherina decided to stay here at home. She was able to balance her running programme with her professional work, under the tutelage of Joe Donnan.

She was often seen running around the local Cavan golf course or the local GAA pitch. It was not until 1994 that she gave up her full-time work to concentrate on running.

Crossing Paths

Catherina's rise to fame ran parallel with the rise of another long-distance runner, Sonia O'Sullivan. Whilst their paths crossed often enough, they remained very different people with different running characteristics. Sonia's path took her towards the college system in the US Catherina's instinct was that you didn't have to travel abroad to be successful.

'Luck was working in my favour when Sonia O'Sullivan emerged on the running circuit at the same time as me. We were born only two days apart. I was fortunate she was around. I wanted to beat Sonia, and she wanted to beat me. That's natural… whether she was from Ireland, France, Germany or Portugal, it made no difference.

'It was friendly competition… never a rivalry.

'I was thankful because she probably did me a favour. I didn't like all that publicity and her achievements took the limelight off me. I could just go about my business and do my training knowing that I wasn't just the main focus. There was two of us in it.

'If it was just one of us, it would have been a hell of a lot more pressure."

Catherina didn't have any fear, and that included Sonia. She was doing her thing. 'It was a mutual respect in an individual sport, because everyone knows just how hard it is.'

Prayer and Conversation

'My mum was very religious. We said the rosary at home, went to Mass frequently and not just on Sundays but also during the week when we could. It was something I grew up with and it was very natural. When I was competing, I aways wore a miraculous medal in my shorts... that gave me comfort and support.

'I also prayed a lot when I was running and competing. I was praying to keep safe, do well and for strength... to keep healthy. I had a prayer book I read a lot. Sometimes, I just had a conversation with God too!

'It was something I just felt was natural.'

Catherina, of course, was meticulous in her training and preparations. But she could balance her hectic life, as well as being able to switch off or concentrate when needed. She matured as an athlete and gradually became more outgoing and comfortable with the media attention she was receiving.

'It just came natural... the will to win. It wasn't something I had to practice. It was a package... of me and a God given talent. The talent had to come from somewhere! Some don't like to say God, but I am okay with it. It was a gift given to me.'

She ran in order to give her best, but she always had a desire to win. 'It sounds crazy but it was easy to move from 10,000 metres to the marathon... as the longer you run, the slower you go. Cross-country and 10ks are very hard, but my genetics helped me cruise at a higher pace for longer.'

Hardship and Awareness

'My favourite prayer is *The Lord is my shepherd*. This prayer has everything for me. I return to it daily.

'During races also, I prayed for strength when I was tired and said to God... "You lift my legs, and I will let them down". This was a mantra that I repeated over and over frequently! I do believe we all have a greater strength that we don't always tap into. I also believe as young people we are not taught enough about our gifts.

'We are more than what we do. I try to live by the fruits of the Holy Spirit... that's my personal insight in my faith.'

She notes that it was a friend who helped her develop an awareness of her spiritual side of life. 'This insight for me came through hardship. When you go through tough times, you look for an inner strength. The challenge is to balance the spiritual life with your whole life. This is a great challenge. The issue for me is, not enough people know about this. Not everyone wants to know this.

'The rat race of life distracts people. There are only a few people that I could relate to and have this conversation with.' She also fondly remembers her mother during her races. 'My mother never wanted to watch a race. She would often go out for a walk and say the rosary on her beads.'

Faith and Judgment

'It was always there. Running is such an individual sport. I could not do it on my own. I was aware that I had this inner power, and it was only a matter for me to let go. We can only do so much. It was a mindset.'

Talking about faith with others runners before races was something that never happened.

'I did not speak to other runners. It wasn't really done, even though I was aware many of the African runners prayed, read their bibles and were very open about it. We don't really live in an environment where we can talk about all these deep questions, about our enlightenment and spiritual paths.

'You can't really talk a lot about our faith... as we get judged.'

Catherina blessed herself before races. 'I often said, "God you help me to prepare for this... and through this. I have trained hard and now I depend on you".'

Looking back, she treasures trips that her family took with her. 'There was one race in Portugal, in the Algarve. My mum was with me, and we had an incident in that her handbag was stolen. I went out, ran... and won. The organisers made a fuss of mum as well as me. She loved it. It is a precious memory.

'Later that Sunday evening we went for a walk to look for a church for Mass. We found one open and lit a candle.'

'When I travelled for races I did try to go to Mass when I could. A memory I have is during the London marathon which took a while... my parents went to Mass during the race. That broke up some of the time for them and settled them.'

Ready to Move On

CATHERINA HAD ENOUGH of competing, and was ready to move on in her life. 'I travelled well and met lovely people. I just loved to run and enjoyed that.' And while she's at peace with the fact that it's all over now, letting go wasn't exactly easy.

'The true self is everything and when we learn to live from there, we will be happy.' Gratitude is important in life, and she is grateful for both the good and the bad. It all shaped her into the person she is today.

'Nobody keeps going forever. It is a short window as well. You only have so many years at that high level... and to be able to put in the commitment and the dedication over that time.' Soon after running she got married and had two children.

'This was the most enjoyable part of my life... the daily routine. I love being a mother. The transition was easy.' She also reflects, 'Running fulfilled you at a point, then children, family life give new meaning to life.'

Looking back, Catherina now has a new appreciation for her life. 'I have a funny relationship with me and my success. There is a lot of living to do when the sport is over. That was part of my life, but I have flourished in being a mother. Success didn't help me overcome challenges. My purpose is to get close to the source of life, freedom from our thoughts... being happy and finding that is important.

'That is the journey that we are all on, that I am on. Our true nature is happiness. When things don't go our way, you realise that the God within us, helps us to keep going.'

•••

Finding New Purpose

'My main running years were the 90s. I started getting tired running around the age of 29. You get worn out, physically and mentally.

'I didn't mind the solo running. For some it was a commitment, but I loved the simple lifestyle. It was not an extra, it was something I did… run, sleep and prepare. The novelty of running internationally soon wears off, as people expect more success. That is pressure.'

'Being a professional athlete you have different traits. I did enjoy my career… the success, the hard training. I loved the racing… competition. People think it is great that I have won the London Marathon, and European titles, but it doesn't do a whole lot for me.

'I am more than that.' She is. Finding her character and who she was became important for Catherina.

'We go through different stages of life. Life is challenging, it doesn't always go the way we would like it to go.

'What made me happy running was the relaxing of the mind and getting closer to the source. The quieting of the mind is what gets us closer to the source. The mind goes quiet… and a freedom occurs, free of thoughts.

'During the intensive phase of running and training, I found I did not personally grow.' Catherina was maturing into her next chapter.

Letting Go

'Of course I am happy to say, I was happy to let go. It was not as easy or quickly as that… letting go was a challenge. You have to let go.

'You have to park it and move on.

'I've done the full circle in that now I can go out for a run in the park and just enjoy it. What I'm doing now with the running classes, with groups of ordinary people, it is all very accessible… some run 5ks and 10ks. Others try to run marathons, though they're not elite athletes. I like dealing with these people because they just want to experience that joy of running, and that feeling of well-being that running gives them.

'I can associate with that.' Not everyone finishes with the same reaction.

'I know that a lot of sportspeople find it hard to let go, but to be honest, that's the reason you can call it egotistic. At the end of the day, the reason why we don't want to let go is because we're not getting that approval anymore.

'There's a long time after your career. As I said, it's only a short window and the ultimate thing for everyone is to be happy. But in every single one of us there is a much deeper part. Our true self. If we think of our true self... which is all perfect, all good, all happy, all loving, all those things... if we can kind of focus in on that, then life is much nicer and much smoother.'

For Catherina, her pure love for solely running shines through always. 'Happiness does not live in fame or fortune. When we are content or happy, that is when we are close to our source.'

She's very thankful for her colourful career and wonderful achievements. She's grateful too for all the help and support from family, friends and everyone else along the way, and she notes that God has been shaping her in her life. However... 'I'd like to be remembered for nothing to do with running. I'd like to help other people more. I'd like to be remembered for me as a person... Catherina.'

She has her wish in a song composed in her honour!

> *On the page of sporting history,*
> *Let's engrave her name in gold,*
> *To children yet unborn*
> *Her noble deeds will be told.*
> *Wherever athletes gather,*
> *With pride they'll speak her name,*
> *And say well done Catherina,*
> *The lass from Cornafean*

●●●

THE
LONELIEST
PLACE
in the world

'I prayed that I would win not just because it meant a lot to me, but because it was so important for so many people. I wanted to win for them, to give them a celebration, something to cheer about in the middle of everything that was going on.'

barry mcguigan

BOXER

BARRY MCGUIGAN WANTED to be more than a boxer. He wanted to heal a whole nation during his blistering career in the ring through the 1980s, and entering the ring under the UN Peace Flag was a recurring message he offered to the warring people of Ireland.

He also could fight with a magnificent passion. His nickname, 'The Clones Cyclone' was not offered him on a whim.

In 1985, in London, Barry became the WBA featherweight champion of the World – importantly, the lineal crown, as he had defeated the previously unconquerable Eusebio Pedroza from Panama. He was very popular with Irish and British audiences, representing neutrality and peace in a time when Ireland, where he lived, was in turmoil with the Troubles. But outside of these islands, his brilliance and his message to non-sports fans, was acknowledged when he was inducted into the International Boxing Hall of Fame in 2015.

Barry came from a quiet Irish town. His parents Pat and Katie had a grocery shop in Clones He was born in 1961 and at the time his parents wanted him called Barry, but there was a local observance that a child's first name should be a Christian or saint's name. A family friend suggested he be called Finbarr, after the patron saint of Cork. Barry was an abbreviation of that! His mother is reported to have said, he will never be called Finbarr again.

One of a family of eight children, the McGuigans were well used to a form of celebrity from an early age as their father was also a well-known entertainer, and had represented Ireland in the Eurovision Song Contest in 1968 (under his stage name Pat McGeegan).

Barry went to the local school in Clones. He was an altar boy, a typically Catholic boy. He also went to Kiltegan when he was 14, just exploring the possibility of the life of a missionary priest. He was nearly sent home as he got into a fight with another lad! He stayed there for two weeks.

At 14 years of age, young Barry started boxing. In 1977, two years later, he won his first national title. He was still a boy, but he was already well acquainted with hard work and discipline. Around 200 people travelled from Clones. His journey had formally begun, and would continue, arriving at Loftus Road in London on June 8, 1985.

World champion!

As an amateur, McGuigan represented Northern Ireland in the Commonwealth Games at Edmonton in 1978, and fought for Ireland at the 1980 Summer Olympics in Moscow. He became a UK citizen so that he could compete for British titles, a path some boxers from Ireland regularly took.

His marriage to his wife Sandra was a mixed marriage. Barry is Catholic and Sandra is a Protestant (Church of Ireland), and also from Clones. It was tough boxing in those years of the Troubles, trying to navigate all the various tensions and traditions. However, he paved a neutral path and attracted fans from every community north and south and later in the UK. The singing of *Danny Boy* at his fights by his father, rather than any national anthem, was another brilliant message to everyone following Barry.

His faith took an important role in his life, and Barry realised he needed to be close to God. He tells a story of attending Mass in Clones and he knew all the words. For Barry, 'religion is a very personal thing', but it is something he was glad of before all of his big fights. When he lost, and failed to come home with a medal from Moscow, the disappointment was intense, and although he turned professional in 1981, he had considered retirement.

His new manager Barney Eastwood, a bookmaker based in Belfast with strong boxing roots, brought him up to meet Fr Salvian Maguire a Passionist priest in the Ardoyne area of the city. Fr Maguire duly brought Barry to meet the Poor Clares, an enclosed Order of Sisters. 'I will never forget that day. They were behind a cage. I struck up a relationship with several of the Sisters. This has continued to the present day.

'They are amazing people.'

Barry has maintained a close relationship with the Poor Clares. He continued to visit them at difficult moments in his life and 'their words are a great support'.

Speaking at a parish novena in Graiguecullen, Carlow, in 2014, Barry linked his sports journey to aspects of his faith.

'I thought I was dedicated,' he told those listening. 'Then I met these women… then I realised I didn't know what dedication meant. These people have given their whole life to God.

'They were such a great example to me. Afterwards, before a fight, I used to go and meet them and pray with them. I'd talk about my fights. They never prayed for me to win, only to be safe. They were amazing people. I am lucky to have them in my life.'

Nineteen million people watched Barry McGuigan that amazing summer's night in 1985,

'I had done all my training and preparation and I had done that by myself, but it was very important to pray that I would win… that I didn't hurt Pedroza in the process, and that I'd come through the fight unscathed. So, I prayed for all that.

'I prayed that I would win not just because it meant a lot to me, but because it was so important for so many people. I wanted to win for them, to give them a celebration, something to cheer about in the middle of everything that was going on. I had to win as much for them as myself and that is what I prayed for.'

Light and Guard and Rule

'I used to go into a fight saying a little prayer to block out the noise to keep me concentrated on what I have to do. It was the prayer I said with the Poor Clares and goes like this, 'Angel of God, my Guardian dear, to whom God's love commits us here… ever this day, be at my side, to light and guard and rule and guide. Amen'.

'It was much routine as anything else,' he accepts, 'something to focus your mind with everything going on.'

Fighting for his Life

THE MOST COURAGEOUS night of Barry McGuigan's life was not one of the fights which brought him to World champion status, or even that memorable evening in London in 1985 itself when he was crowned champ.

In the summer of 1986, in Las Vegas, in the second defence of his World title... that was an occasion when Barry proved himself virtually unconquerable.

He lost the fight and his title, to Texan Steve Cruz, but anyone who was there declared that Barry was the greatest Irish fighter they had ever seen. Not just because he went toe the full 15 rounds against an opponent in the desert, and in air temperature which was recorded at 43 degrees centigrade, but because he refused to concede to every human inclination imaginable.

Afterwards, he was transported to hospital, where he feared for his own life. He implored his good friend, Fr Brian D'Arcy to 'stay with me', afraid that he would suffer the same tragic ending as his opponent so many years before, Young Ali.

'Say a prayer, please,' he had asked those in his corner, each time he stumbled back to his stool. Each time, after the 60 seconds respite, Barry rose from the same stool and fought on, and on.

•••

Barry McGuigan retired in 1989, and quickly forged a successful career on television, commenting on fights all over the world. He worked with Sky TV for 10 years, ITV for four more, and he still works in media. He moved into training and set up a boxing academy in parts of London, for children in underprivileged areas, giving them a chance in life. He also founded and became president of the Professional Boxing Association (PBA). Barry is also the founder and CEO of Cyclone Promotions.

Fr Brian D'Arcy became one of his closest friends and even celebrated his sons' marriages. He was often seen praying with Fr Brian backstage, just before a fight. Sometimes, Fr Brian would say Mass for him in his hotel on the morning of fights. Barry appreciated these moments of prayer and blessing even in the dressing-room.

Boxers, literally, put their lives on the line. He has lived with this knowledge all through his adult life as, after eight wins as a professional, he suffered the awful experience of having one of his opponent's die after a fight. In 1982, he defeated a boxer called Young Ali, who subsequently fell into a coma after the bout. Young Ali subsequently died.

That was one tough blow that Barry had to survive himself, but there have been others. His dad died at 52 years of age, in 1987, after fighting cancer. He was very close to Barry. His brother Dermot took his own life at 34 years of age. His daughter Danika was diagnosed with leukaemia in 1987.

'All the way through this, I questioned my faith... why would I believe in God anymore? I am not different from anyone else.' Danika died in 2019 at the young age of 33. In recent times, he also lost his sister and his sister-in-law. He has really questioned his faith and his resilience to get up again is the true mark of someone with deep roots.

'We all have bumps on the road of life.

'When I have difficult moments, the Poor Clares and Fr Brian were there for me. You try to get on with life, but you never fully recover.

'Who knows what the future holds for anyone?'

Barry is a grandfather now and lives in the south-east of England.

●●●

'The one thing I am certain of is that
you are given one life. I do believe in
something greater than myself. I want to
live this life to the fullest!'

bernard dunne

BOXER

BERNARD DUNNE, LIKE many achievers in the sporting arena, was a lucky man to have a great dad. Brendan Dunne was a huge influence on his son. In his own words, Bernard proudly explains, 'dad was the biggest influence in my life. He was my coach… my father and my role model… and a good guy who just wanted the best for us'. Brendan Dunne had a significant impact on the lives of other young people in the neighbourhood too. He invited many young people to take up boxing in Inchicore where he was a coach. Bernard's dad believed that boxing could teach Bernard and his friends a 'framework for living'.

This guidance and encouragement offered young people an opportunity to learn the value of discipline and respect. 'It gave them an opportunity to do something with their lives,' adds Bernard. 'I was blessed with the people I grew up with in all the streets near where I lived, and all over the greater Clondalkin area.'

Bernard was reared in the west Dublin suburb of Neilstown.

'The greatest place on earth,' he declares! His parents are originally from the Aughrim Street area in north inner city of Dublin. Boxing was strong in Bernard's family. His dad boxed in the Phoenix Boxing Club, near Arbour Hill. His uncle was also a boxer. His parents, Brendan and Angela, moved to Neilstown, a growing suburban area. For Bernard, this was 'home' and more. There were many great people, like Brendan Dunne, who strived to develop their young community.

Neilstown, like other housing estates in Ireland, developed a reputation for anti-social behaviour. In truth, it was an area in need of investment.

However, for Bernard, there was nowhere better to live than Neilstown. He is deeply connected to the community, and his parents and sister still live there. He spends quite a lot of time in the area himself, even though he now lives elsewhere.

Bernard boxed in Inchicore, under his dad's guidance. He was a lover of sport. From a young age he was also actively involved in everything and anything that meant competing, from soccer to gaelic football, but around the age of 15 he decided that he needed to specialise, and choose a sport that was closest to his heart.

'When I thought there was more potential... or something special there in the ring.'

There was indeed!

At amateur level he had 119 wins, and just 11 losses, and won 13 Irish titles, but he also experienced the intense disappointment of not qualifying for the Sydney Olympics in 2000. He turned professional the following year, making his debut in the US, in 2001 in Feather Falls Casino in California. He wanted to base his pro career in the States, and learn from the best in the tough game.

Freddie Roach, a renowned trainer in the Wild Car Boxing Gym, taught Bernard everything he knew and he won his first 14 fights. But Dublin was calling him, and he made the biggest and best decision of his life to come home and claim a World title in front of his own people. He signed up with Brian Peters, who would also later manage Katie Taylor when she turned pro, and a deal was signed with RTE to ensure that all of Bernard's fights were shown live on prime time.

In 2006, he became European Super Bantamweight champion, and soon the World title was in his sights. On Saturday March 21, 2009, Bernard faced the Panamanian champ, Ricardo Cordoba and after 11 gruelling rounds, which included a total of six knockdowns, Bernard was crowned WBA Super Bantamweight champion in front of a packed out 02 arena in Dublin.

American sports channel ESPN declared the contest its 'Fight of the Year'.

A Believer, A Follower

Bernard is from a family who attend Mass regularly. His dad is a practicing Catholic and attends the local parish church which is nearby. Bernard's path is slightly different than his dad's and he describes himself as, 'a believer, a follower, but not an active churchgoer.... but I do believe in something bigger than myself. However, I'm not fully sure what it is.

'Yet, I consider myself a spiritual person.' This is not an uncommon understanding for Bernard's generation growing up in a changing faith environment in Ireland.

'I was brought up Catholic and my kids are also being brought up with the Catholic elements of Baptism, First Communion. These are important parts of our family. It is a sense of values and beliefs... a set of behaviours that I try to live by.'

He fondly remembers, in particular, attending Mass with his grandad. 'Whenever I stayed with my grandad, we went to Mass. Afterwards we'd go to the gym to train. My grandad believed I was the next champion and often told people outside Mass.' His family believed in Bernard. For Bernard, family is a core foundation of life.

'I am blessed with a family network to support me. My dad is still the most important person that influences me. My family made the greatest sacrifices for my achievement.'

Passion and Joy

Bernard has always loved boxing. Boxing is his passion and joy. He loved to box and to train hard. 'I wanted to box. I wanted to compete at the highest level. Sacrifice and choice are not the same. I firmly wanted to be involved in my sport and dedicated everything to it.

'It was almost a sacrifice... but it still was my dream!'

He dreamed from the age of five that he wanted to be an Olympian. His dad had been an Olympian in the 1976 Montreal games. Bernard began to try to create a separate identity from his dad as a boxer. 'My dad is Brendan... I am Bernard. I was sometimes mistaken for him. Once I received an award and the organisers put his name on the trophy. I handed it back and said it wasn't me.'

He acknowledges that it wasn't easy having a dad as your coach and in your corner. As a boxer he needed to train, be disciplined, and look after himself. He was unable to experience rites of passage that other teenagers were experiencing and small and big things, like having a steady girlfriend, were not always possible.

'You think you are missing out. I almost resented my dad for this, but now

Love of the Dubs

BERNARD RESIGNED AS High Performance Director of the Irish Amateur Boxing Association in May 2022, after a conflict with his employers continued since the Tokyo Olympic Games. It was a role he held for five years, guiding amongst others, Kellie Harrington to World fame.

Walking away from the boxers he loved, and a job for which he was a perfect fit, was tough, but it was a decision Bernard felt he had to make.

However, he has been giving of himself to others too since his retirement as a fighter. He was part of Jim Gavin's management team as the Dublin footballers won six All-Ireland titles in succession, and he also took up a role mentoring the Galway footballers who reached the All-Ireland final in 2022, before narrowly losing to Kerry.

'To be able to move from one sport to another and thankfully have some sort of success, it's been a great journey,' he resolved of his association with the Dubs. 'And I'm a fan, I love the boys. I went to their games before I even got involved and they came to my fights.

'I knew a lot of them personally anyway.'

●●●

I can reflect that what he did for me was great, and I am thankful to my dad. I missed out on social nights with my friends. After the Leaving Certificate, for instance, I was training and travelling to Argentina to box. I look back now, and my friends would trade all they did for just one day of what I got to do.

'You don't think about this when you are young. As I look back now... I missed nothing. I lived a full life.'

After the disappointment of the Olympics, Bernard decided that he was going to take control and forge a new path in his life. He went to Trinity college to study. Around this time, he was also getting offers of professional contracts. He faced new challenges as he stepped into the next phase of his adult life, and his resolve was tested. On one occasion, in 2002, he failed a routine brain scan before a fight in New York, when a tiny cyst was discovered, and which threw up the possibility that he would not box again.

'For me, I was on a journey and was happy to go along with it... setbacks meant finding another way forward.'

Digging Deep

Bernard's victory over Ricardo Cordoba for the WBA Super Bantamweight title was the first world championship fight in Dublin for 13 years. It was the pinnacle of a dream... the dream of a five-year-old boy. But, the professional fight world is a precarious business, and six months later, back in the O2 arena he would lose his title in the third round, when the WBA's three-knockdown rule meant that the belt went to the No.1 contender Poonsawat Kratingdaenggym. Six months further down the line, in 2010, Bernard Dunne announced his retirement as a professional fighter.

Looking back, he notes that his skills and gifts in boxing were all hard earned. He can reflect on a moment during the world title fight where he had to dig deep. In his words he recalls hitting the canvas and describes... an 'outer body experience'.

'I had a moment in the fifth round during the world title fight.

'I was on the floor. I had a conversation on the floor about all my life. In what seemed to last about 25 minutes, this conversation in reality lasted about two seconds. The referee was counting me down. My life passed before me.

'I spoke about my family... choices that I made, moving to America... all this time I was on the floor. All the decisions that it took for me to get to be here. I was asking myself questions like, *What was it all for? What was I going to be?*

'I also thought that if I don't get up people would tell me it was simply hard luck or it wasn't meant to be.'

With the whole of Ireland watching this countdown, Bernard also notes his family were beside the ring. He could see his mother's head on his dad's shoulder during the countdown. His mother was praying, holding her rosary beads.

Bernard dug deep and found a deeper resolve to get up. On deeper reflection he now recalls hearing a voice... no, not God's voice, but the voice of his trainer pleading with him to get up. His destiny was the culmination of his life's sacrifice... and Bernard rose from the canvas.

'I vividly remember when I won it, I said it was 'Ours'... for my people. It was not just me... it was my family who had faith in me and I was driven to get up because of their faith in me.'

After the fight and having received some medical treatment in the venue, Bernard visited Ricardo Cordoba in hospital. With Cordoba alone in the hospital, he recalled, 'We had shared something special. I had got through it. We talked and understood each other, and I thanked him for being part of something special with me'.

His achievements are all put in perspective at this point in his life as a 42-year-old. He still has the belt that he won. However, he sees himself as more than a boxer... a son, a dad, a husband. These are the reasons that Bernard got up from the canvas that night in the O2.

Uncertainty

Bernard notes that he does not pray in conventional ways. For him, he reflects on what is going on while he is out walking. He is often 'in his mind' talking.

'I'm not sure if it is God or something. For me... I am not sure.'

Ultimately, Bernard is a family man. His dad is still his biggest influence. Bernard is now enjoying his life post boxing. After losing his title and retiring from boxing, he spent a considerable period visiting schools all around Ireland.

He spoke to young people about his life growing up in Neilstown. He spoke about not letting circumstances dictate his dreams. He challenged young people to reach their potential regardless of where they were from.

After boxing he notes that he did not really have a plan. 'I was lost when I came out of the sport. I had no real purpose or direction. You feel you have no value or other purpose. This is a scary place to be.'

Bernard dug deep, again, and found what he needed to do. With his dad and his wife for guidance, he realised that he was gifted in many ways. His skills were all transferable. All his training, planning, taking instructions and setting goals... all are life skills that can be used in so many other ways. He continued to set new targets and new horizons opened up for him. He returned to college, wrote a television show, learned to speak Irish and returned to sport, giving back.

He loves working with other sports people who have a clear vision and who seek excellence in what they do. It is what he has lived and what he can relate to in others.

'All my life experiences are now helping other people follow their dreams and find their potential. I am now a mentor and helping people on their journey.'

He is still on his path of discovery, however. The Christian values he learned at home from his family still have an influence on him. As he integrates them into his own life, Bernard believes that there is a plan for everyone. He follows the philosophy that everything happens for a reason. It is up to the individual to learn from the experiences and tests encountered in life.

'The one thing I am certain of is that you are given one life. I do believe in something greater than myself. I want to live this life to the fullest!'

Bernard believes in taking everything that life gives you. It is these experiences that can bring an individual to new levels. The boxer must decide to get up or stay down. Bernard is truly more than a boxer.

He would like to be remembered in the following manner. 'I challenged the limits... and challenged life.'

●●●

'I came through all this. God is keeping me strong. I get my strength through God. He brings me through this. Thank God for my faith.'

eamon mcauley

BOXER

EAMON MCAULEY WAS always destined to enter the ring. It was like it was written in the stars, and it helped that he came from serious fighting stock.

Rinty Monaghan was his uncle! Belfast's first-ever world boxing champion, and a man immortalised by a 10ft-high bronze sculpture erected in Cathedral Gardens, close to where he grew up. His grandfather was Harry McAuley, a former professional champion, while his father Patsy won Ulster and Irish titles.

From the Ardoyne area of Belfast, Eamon was born in 1966, just before the Troubles began. But the Troubles provided a backdrop for how his early years were lived. For him, normality was the violence and killings that took place in one of the darkest periods of Irish history. In the street where he grew up, neighbours were shot dead.

His family tried to steer a course, avoiding getting mixed up in the daily drama that was unfolding on the streets of Belfast. 'You never knew what was going to happen next,' Eamon explains. His dad was injured in a car explosion in the city that killed two people. He was also shot a few times.

In 1981, Eamon recalls, during the Hunger Strikes, his best friend being shot on his own doorstep by the British army. 'The Troubles were part of my life growing up, we were stopped, searched, guns pointed at us every other day… it was a normality… we just carried on with life.'

Rocky

Eamon grew up in a house where his family were not churchgoers. However, he does note his granny was very religious. He recalls how she taught and prayed the rosary with him, and brought him to Mass in the local parish run by the Passionist order in Holy Cross.

'When I boxed, I went to confession that day. I got that idea from the *Rocky* films! I did say some prayers. I had total belief in myself in the ring. My prayer was not for victory, but to do my best... not to get injured or humiliate myself.'

During his boxing years, however, he became distant from his faith. God was not really part of his life during this time. Then, in 1995, he attended a weekend retreat organised by Cursilio, an international prayer movement with its roots in Charismatic Renewal. He began to realise he had some faith, but as he later came to realise... he was a 'mechanical' Christian. A mechanical Christian is one who goes to Mass by habit with no real engagement either in listening or participation.

Beginning from that weekend, he attended more faith retreats and began a journey into a deeper commitment to faith. This coincided with the time he was finishing in the ring.

Family Champions

Boxing, of course, was a huge influence in Eamon's childhood. He grew up with all the stories about family members' success. Apart from Boxing, Eamon loved all sport, especially football. In primary school he played with Holy Cross and in 1977 they won the Northern Ireland Schools Cup. He was very talented on the field, and had a trial for Northern Ireland.

After playing well and scoring two goals, he was disappointed that he didn't get picked for the team.

'I quit football that day.' He noted that others told him he was not picked because he was a Catholic, but he never played again. Sectarianism in sport was difficult to navigate for a young lad. He focused on boxing. His dad wasn't really there for him and would die at 58 with Pugilistic Dementia. The blows he took in the ring put him into an early grave.

Eamon had chosen to box with the Sacred Heart Club under the tutelage of Eamon Maguire, and quickly proved his worth and great pedigree, winning county and Ulster titles whilst at the club.

'Boxing is huge in Belfast. Many of the clubs are mixed and, largely, religious identity was not that important. I never grew up with bigotry or sectarianism as I fought, boxed and sparred with people from all sides in the club. I realised they were normal people, even though culturally people were saying different things. Like all sport, boxing crosses boundaries and brings people together.'

In 1982, he decided to try his luck in England. It was a difficult period to be Irish in England due to the political climate that pertained. Eamon worked hard at his sport and tried to make a name for himself. Whilst in Manchester, he began to realise how bad the circumstances really were at home.

In Manchester, he soon was making headlines. The *Manchester Evening News* started to call him the 'Belfast Bomber' as he was knocking out most of his opponents! He had to explain to the paper that he came to England to get away from all those connotations. He stayed in Manchester for two years , winning two national titles.

In 1984, he moved south to London, continuing to become well known in the British amateur ranks. The following year, he won the ABA senior title, becoming the first Belfast man to win it since Jack Garland in 1928. 'I went to the ABA senior boxing championships in 1985. The irony is, I was up against a member of the paratroopers, from the British Army. In my local history and community, the paratroopers and army had inflicted so much pain.

'It put me under huge pressure, because if I got beat I would have been accused for the rest of my life of letting the community down. Anyway, I knocked him out in two rounds and broke his nose in three places! (with my right hand!). We have since become friends… this is the great thing about boxing.'

Eamon was now the number one lightweight in the British Isles. He was also gaining experience by sparring many upcoming professionals, and in 1985 he was invited by Barney Eastwood to watch Barry McGuigan challenge Eusebio Pedroza for the World title in London.

Having represented his country on several occasions and winning over 130 fights, Eamon still had the dream he had as a boy… to be a professional boxer. He turned professional that same year, under the legendary Belfast bookmaker and boxing manager.

Doorway to Peace

EAMON MCAULEY'S MEMOIR began with scribbling random stories in old notebooks, and was a form of therapy for the 56-year-old. Eamon, a doorman of 30 years, has written a book charting his journey from the North Belfast streets to the bright lights of professional boxing.

He is the son of Patrick (Patsy) 'Coco' McAuley, once described in a newspaper tribute as a 'compassionate man with fists of stone'.

'He was involved in street fights. He is a North Belfast legend, but I want people further afield to hear about him. There is one story when the British Army couldn't get a Para to beat him, so they flew over a regimental champion from Germany to challenge him.'

His brother's suicide in 2012 is deeply personal, and is also examined in the memoir. 'His name was Paul. He was three years younger than me and left six kids. They are all doing okay now. We never saw it coming.'

'Eamon McAuley: Fighting to find Peace' was released in 2022.

•••

'Eastwood was a nice man… gave me a good deal… I wanted to stay amateur, but he encouraged me to be professional.' The attraction of being in the same camp and to spar with people like McGuigan, and Dave Boy McAuley and Paul Hodkinson, was huge. 'I now began to feel the pressure of boxing and winning. My family was a family of winners.'

In the Ardoyne, among the older generation, Eamon was always known as Coco's son, as his father had a fearsome reputation as a street fighter.

'Barry McGuigan was there in camp and we sparred with each other. We became friends, it was a wonderful time to be boxing around this time. Barry was a huge influence over me. Barry was the hook Eastwood had to catch me.

'Barry has great faith. He has come through a lot too.' Towards the end of his career, Eamon began to turn towards God for help.

'I only pulled out of one fight… the fight I lost due to an injury. I hurt my foot so I could not plant my feet for punching power. I was in control but it had to be ended. I won more fights after in London. However, no matter how hard I trained, some fights were being cancelled. Sometimes, after months of training… a cancellation… no money.

'It was tough. I just couldn't get the breaks I dreamed of!'

A New Life

Eamon's professional career did not take off as he had dreamed. He won 11 out of 12 fights. He was promised a 'go' at the Irish title. He trained extremely hard and was disappointed that it was cancelled, just days before the fight. He had put so much effort into it. Gradually, he realised his dream was at an end. In time, though, Eamon would return to the sport as a coach with the St John Bosco club in Belfast.

In recent years, he has had some personal family tragedies.

'I came through all this. God is keeping me strong. I get my strength through God. He brings me through this. Thank God for my faith.

'Since I left boxing, my faith has got stronger.'

Since he attended his first Cursillio weekend he has continued to work on his spiritual life and bring this message to other young men. He notes that he still gives thanks to God every morning, and last thing at night. He now attends

Mass, loves to sing and notes that faith has left him in a better place on every level compared to his younger years.

He takes care with both his exercise and diet. He is still connected to boxing via coaching and developing and deepening his knowledge as a boxing historian, and Eamon especially enjoys going into schools and inviting students to watch his videos on YouTube. 'The kids still think I am a hard man!'

He is happy to talk about his life in sport and his faith journey. He is associated with the pro-life movement in his community and spends time with other Christians helping in the community, including aiding the homeless.

'I need to be around holy people... Christians from other traditions. You need to be surrounded with people who are religious. That is important.'

He hopes he will be remembered as, 'A friendly guy, always reaching out... living for the Lord. And not holding grudges.'

●●●

ARM
in arm

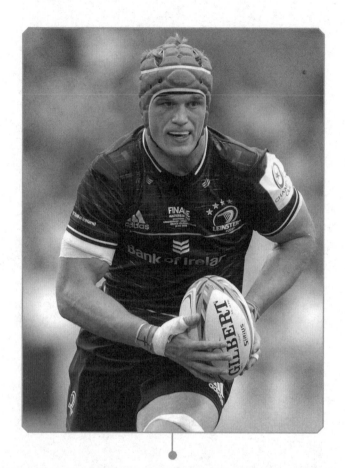

'I find it fascinating that most people associate me as being religious and are intrigued that I have a faith.'

josh van der flier

RUGBY PLAYER

IN THE EARLY summer of 2022, Josh van der Flier was officially in the form of his life. The 29-year-old was named Ireland's Players' Player of the Year, voted on by his peers, and then a week later he was selected European Player of the Year, receiving over 30,000 votes from fans across the continent.

'It's not just been this last year,' stated legendary figure Brian O'Driscoll upon hearing of the flanker's awards. 'It probably started 18 months to two years ago… but the progression has been magnificent.'

And even more was still to come!

When Ireland travelled down to New Zealand, nobody expected the greatest month in Irish rugby history. The All Blacks held a 14-0 record over Ireland in matches on home soil over the last 46 years, but after losing the first test, Andy Farrell's team came back with the most formidable back-to-back displays ever seen in green… and wiped the hosts away with a 2-1 series win.

And the Irish player of the series was the red-capped Josh van der Flier.

In Leinster blue and Ireland green, Josh is living his dream. But it was necessarily destiny, rather the life choice of his grandparents (Johannes and Joke) on his father's side, who are Dutch. They came to Ireland with plans to start a radiator factory in the 1950s, landing first in Finglas, and then moving to Wicklow. His mother is from Kilkenny.

Josh has lived in Wicklow town all his life. It was there he began his love of sport, which grew when he attended Wesley College, a Methodist school, as a boarder in Dublin for six years. He was quiet as a boy in school and was small, and started his career as a scrum-half.

'I enjoyed the ethos of the school... there was a good atmosphere... a good place to be. I was lucky to have been able to go there. There were opportunities for everyone to do well.' Josh continued his education in recent years, attending Dublin Business School while forging his Ireland career, and earning a first class Masters in Business Administration.

Scripture and Ball

'Each Sunday we would go to the local church, which is Church of Ireland in Wicklow. Mum and dad would take time to read some bible stories to us from those children's books. We also had prayer every mealtime to bless the food. I also prayed before I went to sleep. Prayer was an integral part of our family at home and growing up.'

Dirk van der Flier, who had played rugby for Old Wesley and also for Leinster under-21s, and his wife were also involved with Scripture Union, a non-denominational Christian organisation. His mother helped to run summer camps for young people and at one time his dad was chairperson.

Scripture Union has a property near Avoca, Co Wicklow (Ovoca Manor) which was used for residential trips for young people, mainly from Wicklow and Dublin.

'Both my parents were involved with Scripture Union for many years. I remember going as a child to Ovoca Manor where my parents would be helping with a primary school adventure weekend camp. I was too young to join, but I took advantage of the sports hall to kick a ball with my brother... other opportunities too!'

These camps were simply fun, with some religious activities. 'Many of the young people were mad for the sports aspects, but there were some fun games and some reflective quiet moments when it was quite normal to have talks and discussions. It was all natural and normal.'

'It made an impact on me. All my upbringing involved faith... Sunday School or opportunities for kids to be part of prayer.'

As a teenager it can be tough to express faith, due to pressure from peers. Josh came home from boarding school at weekends and joined his family in church. 'I found it hard early on to talk about faith. I still do. It does not come natural to me like others… telling people about my faith.

'I am a private and quiet person.'

Josh found ways to navigate his teenage years and his personal faith. As he got older, he values time to reflect. 'It's not often you get time to focus on questions of personal faith and values.'

A Ball in his Cot

'I only played cricket, hockey and rugby in school… all team and structured sport.' He focused on rugby, but had little choice, remarking that as a baby his dad had put a rugby ball in his cot! 'Rugby was a huge thing for me. Dad loved to teach us and played with us in the garden.'

Around the age of 14, he decided to take the game extra seriously, paying attention to the smallest details. 'I was competitive and wanted to be better. I asked my coaches how to do parts of my game better… or to show me and teach me to try different things.'

In his fourth year at school, he notes that he researched online how to do personal gym sessions. 'I then did around nine gym sessions per week to be better… and bigger! I was training hard to try to get on the senior team at Wesley.' His dedication got him there.

'Even now as a professional, we only do half that amount of gym sessions. My training regime in school didn't make sense, but it was what we were trying to do, better ourselves and our game.'

He graduated from the senior team in Wesley and had a few trials for Leinster, but it was not until sixth year that he was picked for the Leinster under-19 team for a summer programme.

The following summer he played for Ireland's under-19s. This pattern of constant improvement continued until he got selected for the Leinster Academy 'When I left school, I had played with UCD… unless I was playing with the Leinster teams.'

Making the Line

JOSH, WHO WAS called up to the Irish squad by Joe Schmidt for the Six Nations Championship in 2016, has crossed the line for seven tries in his Ireland career to date. The first came in year two, in June 2017, against Japan on tour and he scored against Japan again four years later. In between, his first Six Nations try was against Wales in the Aviva Stadium in February 2020 .

He scored again, against Argentina, in the Aviva in 2021, and there were two more tries in the Six Nations the following season – one against the French in the Stade de France, and one more at home to Scotland.

Then came Wellington in July 2022, when his try helped propel Ireland to a famous win and a series victory over the All Blacks.

●●●

It's in the Detail

'I have loads of little parts of detail that are part of my preparation. I listen to beat music… loud and pumped-up before a game. As I drive to the game I play calm, religious worship music… reflective music that calms me down. The peaceful music is just like going to church. It offers me that important moment of calm.

'My youth pastor would always tell me, 'You can honour God by playing rugby'. I know God gave me a gift and I honour that by playing to the best of my ability.' I have always loved rugby and dreamed of being professional. God blesses you if you work hard at something. I bring my passion for sport and connect that with my passion for God.

'Before a game… and this can be in the dressing-room or the night before, or even on the pitch… I say a prayer. Sometimes I have prayed with my fiancée (now wife) before a match. It is not an exact prayer, but along the lines of thanking God for the opportunity… and to honour God in how I play and act.

'I find it fascinating that most people associate me as being religious and are intrigued that I have a faith. Sometimes in the physio room there have been chats with other lads, who might quietly disclose that they go to Mass too.

'I have seen lads very nervous before a big game… whether it is Leinster or Ireland, or even club… and they bless themselves. Or they have their eyes closed… some even kneel down in prayer. I have seen many different moments like this.

'Obviously, there are more people than just me praying!'

Some of these people may not naturally fit into the faith category. Faith is normal to Josh, but for others it is an even more private matter. 'I suppose it might be Irish culture… to keep your faith private. It's very different to other players from overseas, who are very open and expressive about their faith.

'I wear a cross on my wrist. I like it for myself… a reminder that God is there. It is not a tattoo, but in the form of tape and a marking. When I was in school there were not too many students open about their faith, if they had any. I remember watching big international games and I'd see the odd player with a cross on their wrist.

'This was very encouraging to me, to know there are other Christians playing sport.' Just like the gladiators in the Colosseum fighting the early Christians, maybe Josh can inspire a new generation of gladiators to do their best on the pitch.

'I used to live in a house with a group of lads, but I'd go home each weekend and would attend my local church. During the Covid-19 restrictions, I followed some of the online church services. I also am happy attending a Catholic church with my wife and her family, if I am around at weekends.'

Josh and his wife have a strong faith. They are from different faith backgrounds but with a commitment to faith. 'I am comfortable in both traditions. We have always prayed together, and it is important to both of us. She and my mother pray before my games.'

Sacrifice and Ambition

Josh has, like his peers on the Leinster and Ireland squads, put his rugby career ahead of a social life. 'My dream was to get to the higher level. Everyone is different, this was the way I had to do it.

'There are definite sacrifices, but I am always so grateful to play for Ireland and to be in the Leinster squad for many years. It was harder in my teens… looking back, I was so determined to do well… I missed out on parties, celebrations… and nights out. I came from a lesser-known school and had to work harder to get noticed in rugby.

'I might have made the sacrifices, but would I have made it if I had not made the sacrifices? I don't think so. My choices have made me achieve where I am today.

'Rugby has gone well for me… playing for Ireland is an incredible honour. I have appreciated it, especially so when I was injured, and I know it is a huge deal for my family and friends. Being in the same Ireland camp with some of the modern legends of Irish rugby was an eye-opener, but being in "the bubble" with such a talented group of people around you also meant that you played at a higher level.'

Standing on the pitch and hearing *Ireland's Call*, he notes is a, 'crazy experience… just trying to keep your focus on the game means keeping you emotion in check'.

He does not take for granted anything he has achieved to date. In a professional game, every player is only as good as his next performance, and judgment on every player can be brutally tough. He still has ambition to play at the highest level for many more years. 'I would love to play more in the Six Nations… the next World

Cup, and there are going to be so many big European matches with Leinster.'

Amongst his teammates, Johnny Sexton stands out for his leadership but every other player in the Leinster and Ireland squad are the ultimate professionals, in Josh's eyes. Josh has now completed his formal studies, and has taken up French to speak socially with his fiancé and her family. He found being able to learn a new language a good distraction from the weekly pressures of the game during peak season.

He has not really focused on what he will do when his playing career is over. However, he acknowledges, that God will reveal something for him.

There is no fixed plan. 'I see the hand of God guiding me. God works everything for the good… I believe this. I see how God has created this path I am on now. It is up to me to try to make the most of the opportunities that have been given to me.'

He would like to be remembered as Josh.

'I hope it is nothing to do with rugby. I'd like to be remembered for who I am, rather than just the sport I played. Maybe how I made people happier or impacted on them.'

●●●

'Through all the success and failure,
hopefully my character will be seen. With
God by my side, I can face the future with
confidence both on and off the field.'

lena tice

HOCKEY PLAYER

ELENA 'LENA' TICE was hardly allowed time to dream.

At 13 years and 272 days she made her debut as a senior international cricketer. Lena was the second youngest player in the history of the game, male or female, to do so! In 2014, she represented Ireland at the ICC Womens' World Twenty20. By 17, Lena was a dual Irish hockey and cricket international.

The next year, she played for Ireland in the World Cup final.

Luckily, Lena was ready to take on the world with the help of her childhood experience. Her father George is a veterinary surgeon and, working for a multinational food production company, he and his wife Scarlett enjoyed living in many different locations as they reared their family of three (Lena has two brothers, Patrick and Dalton, both of whom have also excelled at sport).

Lena was actually born in Basingstoke, in Hampshire in England, but the family moved to Indianapolis when she was four, and to Vienna when she was six. Two years later, they relocated again, settling in Scarlett's home village of Glenealy in Wicklow.

'I was an international kid growing up, with lots of influences,' Lena admits. 'Mum is Irish and dad is English, so I have a real hybrid accent as a result of living all round the world as a youngster!'

She attended school in Aravon in Bray, and later St Gerard's School also in

Bray, which in turn has led her to studying economics in UCD. From an early age she was always playing sport with her father and brothers. 'Dad just treated me equally like the boys. We played a lot... I have had an amazing amount of support from my family.

'I started to play cricket from around the age of nine, and at 10 I was playing with Merrion Cricket Club in Dublin. My career started off from there!'

Sunday School

'I grew up in a Christian family and my memories revolve around going to church, and other Christian families. From an early age, I understood who Jesus Christ is, I understood what the bible was and what it means to pray and read scripture. Faith... it has always been there in my life.

'I also attended Sunday School both here in Ireland and also in those huge mega churches in the United States. I have been part of smaller churches too, both in Vienna and in my home church in Redcross, in Wicklow.'

Lena played cricket to begin with, heavily influenced by her dad. Her summers in Vienna were actually spent at the crease. 'That's where my love of cricket comes from!' Despite making her international debut at 13, in her teens she was combining her passion for both cricket and hockey.

'I combined both for as long as I could. When I was 17, I had to choose.' Hockey was picked as her primary sport. 'What happened was, I was in my Leaving Cert year, and I had played cricket solidly up to this point, but I was also getting much better at hockey.' Her realisation that she could not play dual sports, and do well at her final school exams, left her with a pending decision.

'I decided just to play hockey for my school and club, and during the year I got my first senior cap. As a result, I didn't get back to cricket.

'Even though I am finishing off my finals in college, my sport will be my career. It is difficult because as a female athlete you don't make a lot of money!' She desires to be successful in sport but understands she will have to have some options outside of hockey to keep herself secure. 'I'll push for that recognition.

'I want to play professional sport... it's my dream!'

Lena states that her faith is not just for Sundays. When she travels with teams, she makes time to pray and connect with others in her faith. 'My Christian faith is not just on Sunday and a few prayers. It is everything to me, even if I don't always live it out well... it's my identity.

'It is for every single day.'

All her teammates know her faith is important to Lena, and that Christian identity is something that leads to discussion with her fellow players. 'I also have some teammates who are committed Christians. There are others who are not, which is fine.'

Winning silver at the World Cup in 2018 is, to this point, her crowning memory. 'That was my highest achievement... and amazing.' But Lena has also has been part of teams that have experienced failure, and remembers not winning a game playing for Ireland in the cricket World Cup in 2014.

'There are times I have lost games for my team. I have experienced disappointment in my career, but this only makes you stronger. When the tough moments come, you dig deep and draw on all that hard work you have done.

'Then you can push on.'

Granting Peace

'At the end of the day I am not viewed differently by God if I succeed or fail... this makes a huge difference. I am only human. It is natural at times to be disappointed. When I get time to reflect and sit down and think, I can get peace from the reality that my identity is in Christ and I am still perfectly loved by him!'

Lena often prays intensely in the lead up to games. 'In the dressing-room, prayer for me is a big deal. I don't pray that I can be better than my opponents or that I can play well. I am a person who gets anxious in these highly charged moments. Prayer is what I use in order to be at peace in these times.

'It helps with my nerves. I know that even if I play poorly, it is not the end of the world.'

She acknowledges that it is hard to put words on this, especially when you want to succeed and play well. A favourite quotation that inspires her is, "Present your request to the Lord and he will grant you peace beyond all understanding".

'I have found peace like no other when I have asked God for peace.' This is what Lena draws on in the dressing-room. When she doesn't pray, this can lead her to have increased anxiety. 'Prayer before a match gives me a sense of peace, so

Pushing on to Paris

BECAUSE OF COVID, Lena and her teammates on the Irish hockey team did not make it to Tokyo for the Olympic Games until the summer of 2021. There, especially after waiting for 12 months to experience the ultimate sporting dream, they met with disappointment in not being able to medal.

Lena, however, was one of the standout performers. She was a pillar of the team's defence and marked herself down as a permanent member of the Girls in Green for many years to come.

As she says, 'Disappointment only makes you stronger. When the tough moments come, you dig deep and draw on all that hard work you have done.

'Then you push on.' Paris 2024 is in Lena's diary!

•••

I'm aware that I lean on my faith at those times.'

I am far from perfect. There are times I forget to pray. However, I only find this peace in my prayer life and relationship with God.'

Lena's achievements have come at a price. She has sacrificed parts of her life for sport and as a result has missed friends' weddings, and holidays together. However, she would not change anything. 'All those sacrifices, going training and so on, have led me to where I am today. I have chosen to live my life this way. It's what I want to do.

'I have made sacrifices in my life and missed out on normal activities, but it is not a sacrifice... my sport is something I love doing.'

She has various mentors who have helped her in her sporting career. One of her role models is Katie Taylor. 'She is one of the best Irish athletes ever... full stop. I'd love to meet her. The way she has integrated her faith into her sport! She is such a competitor and fighter.

'It is great to see Katie talk about her faith... it is reassuring that you can put your time into sport and it doesn't take away from your time with God. It's awesome she speaks openly. I would find that difficult. To have a sister in Christ playing at that level is amazing.'

Dreaming of More

Her dream is set on a successful playing career and being a role in sport at the end of her career. 'I want to help to progress the game and bring it forward for girls coming behind me. I want to see hockey fully professional, and I want to have a career in sport post playing.' Meanwhile, Lena lives her faith in an open manner. She recalls that during the World Cup final, before each game she drew a cross on her left forearm as a representation of her faith. 'My faith is more important than hockey, because it is what will remain. God's love for me doesn't change if I do well or I don't do well. That's faith.'

'God has guided me one hundred percent in sport. There are so many times that He has been part of my life. I only can recognise this as I reflect and look back!' She takes inspiration from the quote "I can do all this through him who gives me strength". (Philippians 4:13)

Lena finds it nourishing being in church. 'I get guidance from the church I attend… a small church in Dublin. There are people there who look out for me, and pray with and for me.

'I would love to be remembered as being a really good player and for honouring God in how I played and conducted myself… even though I have fallen short.' Her mum's words of advice also resonate for her… "At the end of the day all that matters is your character".

'Through all the success and failure, hopefully my character will be seen. With God by my side, I can face the future with confidence both on and off the field.'

●●●

'I feel like my faith is something that is so individual, it's never measured against another human being. It's where I don't feel vulnerable. It's where a lot of my self-worth and a lot of my understanding of what is important to me, what I want to achieve in life, comes from.'

— Jenny Simpson

American Middle Distance Runner and Steeplechaser

'Sportspeople are quite selfish. You are so driven and focused on yourself. Yet, I still got on my knees... I needed help. It was all one-way. I was not giving anything back. I only wanted God to help me, but on my terms.'

kyle mccallan

CRICKET PLAYER

KYLE McCALLAN WOULD march through a top flight cricket career which would culminate in him becoming Ireland's most capped player. He announced his retirement from the International game in December 2009 after receiving a record 226 caps. He also captained Ireland 54 times. The right-hander and off-spin bowler scored 3,616 runs at an average of 23.33, and he also took 256 wickets. Such commanding figures make it all look relatively simple for Kyle, but, of course, they only tell half of his story.

The other half is the story of a boy and man who had to grow into the towering figure who become known as Kyle McCallan, Irish team captain.

And every great story has bumps on the road.

Kyle had made his Irish debut in 1996. The following year he was selected for the ICC Trophy (which was the name for the World Cup qualifying tournament at that time). He travelled to Malaysia and spent, as he says himself, the next four weeks 'carrying drinks!'

'I had trained so hard to get out there, was in good form… in fact the best shape I'd ever been in,' he reveals. 'But it turned out I was the one guy who didn't get a game the whole tournament. I probably felt a bit sorry for myself, but looking back I should have done a bit extra to try and get into the team. Instead I accepted that I wouldn't be picked.

'Added to that, my parents had paid a lot of money to go to KL (Kuala Lumpur) so it was disappointing for them not to see me play. It did teach me one lesson... never to take selection for granted. After that, I was determined I would never go through that experience again and maximise what I have.'

Done!

Three years later, he was appointed Irish captain. At his third time of asking, in 2007, he played in the World Cup, when Ireland splashed onto the world stage with a draw against Zimbabwe in their first match, and then brilliantly defeating Pakistan next time out.

'Pakistan was the game everybody talks about but I still have a vivid memory of a disastrous first game against Zimbabwe. The first ball that came to me, it went through my legs for four, I didn't bowl particularly well and got a duck, and would admit I froze on the big stage,' he notes.

'But things turned around and we ended up having a brilliant tournament. We had the opportunity to enjoy eight weeks in the Caribbean.'

In the Blood

Kyle, from Carnmoney in Antrim, was awarded an MBE in 2010 for his services to cricket.

That service began as a small boy. He adored the game from an early age and soon was recognised as a prodigious talent, playing underage cricket with Ulster 15s. 'By the time I was 18 I was playing with the Ireland development squad.

'My family are originally from Sion Mills, in Tyrone... cricket is in the blood. I started playing when I was 12 and got involved and made my way quite quickly in the game. I started at Ballyclare, where I met John Solanky (the Tanzanian great who formerly played for Glamorgan)... my aspirations were to play for Cliftonville 1st XI. Representative cricket was just a natural progression. When I had played for Ulster and then Irish Schools I certainly aimed to play for Ireland.'

He made his Irish debut at 21 years of age.

Kyle's family were part of the Christian Brethren tradition. His parents were church-goers and they ensured Kyle took part in his faith, which included from an early age being sent to Ballyduff Gospel Hall. His personal recollection from church was that there was not a lot of 'grace' preached at the time. It was Christian but did not feel it. It was very conservative. 'There was a lot of talk about hell. There was not a lot of the love and mercy of God being preached there.'

Here he also attended Sunday school and he got to know his best friend Johnny Lowe. They have been friends all through his school years and to the present.

He became a Christian when he was aged 13. 'This was around the same time I was getting going with my interest and passion for cricket. The church I am from is part of the Plymouth Brethren (or Assemblies of Brethren, a low church and non-conformist Christian movement whose history can be traced back to Dublin at the beginning of the 19th century).

'It was hard-line, and was both traditional and conservative in its teaching. Basically, there was a tension between church and sport. I found myself from an early age getting recognition for my sport and then getting invitations to go on tours to play all over Ireland... and then international games. Cricket became all-consuming for me taking over my weekends... Saturday Sunday. Basically, in my mind, I was being told I could not be a church-going Christian... and a sportsperson and international cricketeer.'

Kyle was at a crossroads. The message he heard was one of fear and for a 15-year-old it was a very austere message. These are real memories for him. As a teenager he had a great awareness of the possibility of hell. That was *the message*. 'Also, for me the message was cricket and sport were of the world... and not of God. The worldly behaviours were not the behaviours of Godly Christians.' This was not good at all for a young man in the making who happened to be sporting mad, playing rugby, golf and anything else that ignited his competitive instincts.

This was a huge challenge for Kyle. Gradually, he prioritised his sport. In turn his commitment to sport superseded his commitment to attending church. From his late teens to his early twenties, Kyle's drift from faith continued. At the same time he was gaining many more honours playing the sport he loves.

He notes, as he was driven towards success in his sporting career, he took defeats and failures hard. 'When cricket and success become your idol, it becomes the be-all and end-all when things do not go well. I wasn't a pleasant person to be around in general!'

Balance and perspective were needed.

Shoulder-to-Shoulder with Greatness

EOIN MORGAN WAS batting in his first one-day international for Ireland. He was 99 not out. At the other end Kyle McCallan was playing his 141st game for his country. It was August 2006, and Morgan and McCallan were at Cambusdoon cricket Ground in Ayr.

'It was the start of the last over and we spoke in the middle and I said. "I'll go, if you go" to get him his century. He played the ball into the offside and I took off, but immediately realised there was never a run. But Moggy responded and when I turned back, he had to go back as well but had no chance of making it.

'So I suppose, looking back, it was my fault. But I can write about that in my autobiography – I ran out the future England captain on 99!' All that time ago, Kyle was sure that Morgan would realise his boyhood dream and would one day play for England.

'He was very ambitious, he made no bones about it and the guys respected him for that,' says McCallan, who was played in 51 of Morgan's first 52 games for Ireland. The only game Kyle missed was when he was on honeymoon with Lynne!

•••

Cricket and Christ

Kyle married Lynne in 2004 and they attended church, St John's in the parish of Kilclooney, in Armagh. The rector was Neville Hughes. 'He was a great preacher and he made an impact on me.' Kyle knew that cricket had given him 'riches', but he still felt spiritually poor.

He had achieved everything he could in sport.

He recalls, on one occasion, being booked into a five-star hotel in Bangladesh, but despite the luxury all around him, it was the poverty of the place that struck him hardest. 'I felt poor at that point. I went back to the hotel.... got on my knees and prayed for forgiveness for my selfishness. I prayed for reconciliation... and to come back into His kingdom.

'I wanted to try to use what He had given for His glory... rather than my glory.'

In 2007, he went to the World Cup in the West Indies. 'We had the famous experience there. The best that cricket could offer. After a few days, the feeling of joy went away. I was left thinking... *Is that it?* I had achieved everything I could from cricket.'

As he looked around him, he noticed that not all the players were happy with everything that was happening to them either. Kyle then noticed that, 'God was speaking to me, or at least I began to notice that God was speaking to me, if I am honest.' He also began to wonder if there was more to life. This period of searching and questioning his faith continued until 2009, when he was on that trip to Bangladesh.

'The complete poverty of the people that I met... this was my wake-up call. I had drifted away from the Church and from God. I had not lost my faith. It was just that I had felt that I could not do the two simultaneously. It was there that I reconciled.

'In many ways, I wish things could have been different.' Around this time Kyle would describe himself as 'part-time' Christian. 'I never lost my faith in God... I kept going to Him when I needed help. I was selfish.

'Sportspeople are quite selfish. You are so driven and focused on yourself. Yet, I still got on my knees... I needed help. It was all one-way. I was not giving anything back. I only wanted God to help me, but on my terms.'

Letting Go

When he returned to Ireland he recalls his wife, unprompted, asking him to attend a series of scripture talks in their local church. He notes that God was beginning to become 'more important to me in everything that I did'. They also talked and realised they wanted to reconnect more to their faith and their church.

'After my return to faith his teammates were curious and often had quiet conversations with me over a coffee.' Kyle was happy to talk about his faith. He does acknowledge that some of his teammates had different levels of faith, however, there was extraordinarily little expression of that in the dressing-room. At the same time, he points out that while there was little prayer in the dressing-room.... 'I played against and with guys who had a strong faith. You could see it in them'.

Everyone has their own rituals before a game. 'I was a little superstitious. I always put my left pad on before my right when getting ready to bat. I liked to bowl with sunglasses on, irrespective of the weather, but perhaps the worst was that when I scored runs, I never cleaned my socks or underwear until I failed!'

Kyle tries to be Christ-like in as much of his life as he can, that is his mission. He sees this as a personal mandate within cricket. 'I prayed before every game. I never prayed for success... just for God to do his will.'

Salt and Light

He made the big decision to retire from the game in 2009. Everyone tried to talk him out of it. And he acknowledges that he was playing the best cricket of his life at this stage. 'The shackles were off. I was playing and enjoying it. I was playing for the glory of God... not me. I gave my best to be 'salt and light' everywhere on the pitch and in the changing room.'

But Kyle knew it was the right decision. He had prayed about it. Family circumstances also confirmed to him it was time to retire. He knew it was time to focus on other things.

'I don't regret it. Of course, I miss it. It was the clearest decision I have made... the decision was made for me by God.'

Kyle also acknowledges that even in his school he was surrounded by good Christians. Andy Gibson, who is now a pastor in CFC Church was a PE teacher there. There was Johnny Young and a student teacher called Nathan McConnell… but Andy Gibson became a big influence on his life.

In Waringstown, in Down, he is encouraged and challenged to reach out to players who play cricket. Kyle is now playing because he wants to be an influencer on the pitch and with other players.. He sees the club as a secular type of church and he feels a responsibility to be there as an active Christian.

'I am still playing sport in my forties. The reason is, I see it is an opportunity to bring God into the changing room in Waringstown. It is my opportunity now after years of being selfish to change from being a one-way Christian, taking from God… to give something back to God. I can now use my experience in cricket to also bring people to God hopefully.'

Kyle is a believer that everything he has done in his life, on the pitch and off it, was part of God's plan for his now faith-filled life. 'It doesn't matter where you have been, it is about where you are going and where you end up.' He acknowledges his colourful past and his present life are in contrast.

He tells the story of a coach telling him that his behaviour towards others was out of order and he needed to change. He regrets how he did not listen to some of the wise counsel he received in his early playing days.

His life is a busy one still, but family comes first, Lynne who was once described as 'long-suffering Lynne' but no more, and children Matthew and twins Rachel and Katie. He now does punditry on Sky Sports, where he enjoys getting to work with some of the greatest former players in the game. He continues, of course, to play for his club, and coaches his school Lurgan College where he is vice-principal. He also attends his local Baptist Church in Portadown.

'The nearer you draw to God, the closer he is to you.' God is now a priority for Kyle. He has a constant awareness of God's presence in his life. He would like to be remembered as the person who relied on God, quoting St Paul, 'I can do all things who does things in me!'

●●●

'I am not an atheist. I do lean
towards the lower end of belief, if
that makes sense. I believe the values
of God can enhance everyday living,
but I don't have it all figured out.'

ian mckinley

RUGBY PLAYER

AT 20 YEARS of age, Ian McKinley's life was turned upside down. And his career as an emerging professional rugby player with very serious promise?

It looked over, no doubt about it. A stray boot in a club game left him with no sight in his left eye. The devastation which wrapped itself around the young man appeared total. Now, zip forward a little over 10 years.

We have all had our lives thrown upside down because of a pandemic which killed hundreds of thousands on every continent, and sought to wreck lives in a multitude of other ways, Ian McKinley included. He was playing rugby for the Italian side Benetton Trevisio since 2016, but in 2021 he was forced to retire a second time when the club was forced to release a clutch of players from their contracts.

A 10-year career in Italy was, suddenly, over. But adversity has been something the Dubliner knows too well. In an amazing decade, and a storyline which would be ideal for any movie script, Ian managed to have seventy percent of the sight in his damaged eye restored, as he played through a professional rugby career that included nine appearances for Italy on the international stage, with a pair of specially built goggles to offer him protection in the thunderous life of a rugby pro.

Ian reviews his life now, and only speaks of opportunity. 'I would not be speaking Italian if I had lived in Ireland. I would not have been exposed to everything that has been so positive for me in Italy.' He was injured in 2010, and retired the following season.

'Ultimately, I made the decision in 2011 to retire. I moved to Udine when I was 22 and not knowing the language was tricky. You certainly learn a lot about yourself. You basically sink or swim in those situations. I adapted, so I'm forever grateful I made the decision to move to Italy. I've made friends for life.

'People have said to me, "You were on course for this great career in Ireland", and I was dealt that hand. Other people are dealt their hand and they have to get through whatever problems they've faced. For me, it opened up the world.'

A GAA Career

Ian grew up in Taney parish in Rathfarnham. Uniquely for him, he grew up in a Church of Ireland rectory, not it seemed anything but quite normal for him. His dad, originally from Tipperary, was a Church of Ireland priest in Tainey and Whitechurch, in Dublin. His grandad was a priest in Templemore.

Ian has always been passionate about sport but, 'I wanted to play rugby from about the age of five. I grew up in a rectory and we had a large space out the back which was big enough to play with a ball... usually a rugby ball. Rugby was always on a Sunday and this was an issue. On Sunday in our family... you went to church and didn't play sport.'

It was then suggested to him that in order play sport he might take up GAA? 'I didn't know the rules, it was just something I watched. I went up to Deerpark and started playing with Kilmacud Crokes, and I loved it. I was fairly young at this stage. I joined up and we went on to win our first Feile (festival) in 2004 with the under-14s and there were many GAA stars to come out of that team, especially Rory O'Carroll who had such a brilliant career with Dublin.'

But Ian comes from a family with strong roots in rugby. His mother Pam played hockey, but his dad Horace played for Trinity and Old Wesley rugby clubs. Pam's dad had played for Wesley in two schools cup finals.

He continued to play GAA with Kilmacud and even played for the Dublin under-16s. In secondary school he played rugby which was weekday... weekends were for GAA. He was also on the Leinster panel from the age of 15. Around the age of 17, he had to choose... rugby or gaelic football?

The challenges of growing up in a Church of Ireland house presented the dilemma of balancing sport and church. He was able to play rugby with school during weekdays and Saturday with his club. Sunday became a rest day from sport... Sunday was a day for church and family.

Ian attended church up to the age of 18. His dad ensured they all attended the church where he was the rector, but gradually, the pressure to attend church and make his own choices was allowed by his parents.

A Buzzing House

He comes from a family with four siblings. The oldest three are close in age, then there is a gap of nine years to Ian. For him it was normal for parish meetings to take place in the house. At home he remembers meetings, events and even the local school had the sports day in their large garden. The school was a Church of Ireland school that his dad had a strong role in helping to build up.

'Our house was always buzzing, people looking for help... looking for direction in faith, money... or trying to reach out to people. Local meetings in the house... you could hear everything in the house. If I was having dinner, I'd make sure not to disturb the parishioners by going into the kitchen with my plate!'

He also notes that beside their garden and sports field was a local graveyard, with Moravian burials (people buried standing up). It was normal for people to ask to walk through their garden to visit the graveyard.

Sundays were also important in his childhood. He remembers that even though he went to a Church of Ireland school, St Columba's in Rathfarnham, after a week of school, daily church services and assemblies the last thing he wanted to do on a Sunday was more church! Yet it had to be done. He attended school on Saturdays also, unlike other local schools... and even Sunday school in his dad's parish. 'As I got older, the last thing I wanted was more church... as we had church services daily in school! Our service was 10.30 in the morning so dad would wake me up at 10am. Mum sang in choir. Dad was the priest. At 13 I wasn't fully connected with what was being taught or talked of by dad. It was normal for me to see my dad robed up, saying a service, praying at the table or with each of us. It was normal for our family.

'At the age of 18, dad led me go in my own direction in discovering faith and practising it. In fact, all four of us have very different beliefs and attitudes to practicing faith.' His brother Philip, has recently received ordination, keeping the tradition of priests in the family alive.

'My parents just encourage me to do what I feel comfortable with and there is never real mention of me attending church.' He appreciates the role his parents have allowed him, to grow in his own understanding of faith and choices, and admits to only really attending church when he visits his parents.

He loves to hear his dad preach. 'I love to listen to my dad. He's a great preacher and I do look forward to hearing him preach when I get the opportunity. When I was younger, I didn't appreciate it but I do realise the value in it for life skills and living your life.'

Ian still believes in... 'something'... maybe it's God.

'I am not an atheist. I do lean towards the lower end of belief, if that makes sense. I believe the values of God can enhance everyday living, but I don't have it all figured out.'

Playing, Platitudes Praying and Injury

In 2010, Ian was playing for UCD against Lansdowne in the All-Ireland league. A teammates boot caught him in the eye whilst in a ruck. After playing six times for Leinster, he was forced to retire from rugby. After this retirement, he moved to Italy to work as a coach for junior sides.

'When I got my injury, I did not blame God for getting the burst eyeball. There are people in the world who have it harder. However, I was almost put off by people saying things like, "God will provide for you". It could be argued they are correct, but for me, I worked my ass off to get back. I don't think God was out doing six hours of fitness. My doggedness was nothing to do with God.'

Ian, naturally, has strong feelings about this time. He didn't need to hear the pious platitudes. All of these episodes led to a near breakdown in 2013 when his brother and him had a heart-to-heart. 'What angered me was when people said God has a plan, when something was so raw. I just thought... *How do you know?* This was not what I needed to hear. It was real anger that lingered for a long time.' He did appreciate people who were praying from him and sending him notes of support. However, he does not think God intervened to help him.

'I don't buy into all that. You must work hard to get anything in life. You need luck and great people around you. My brother Philip spoke to me post injury, when I told him I'd like to get back to playing rugby. We have different viewpoints. He asked me did I think it's God working through me to help in order to get back to professional rugby? I have a different view. Some people turn to God in difficulty. That's not me. For me, my brother was helping me, doing something for his brother. That's all.'

Ian does acknowledge that for some players, they turn to their faith and pray before games. Some of his international colleagues would gather in prayer together. This was not his way. Before leaving for his Italian debut, 'I looked at myself in the mirror and just looked up to say, "today will go well"... and then closed my eyes and said the same thing.'

Whilst he says he does pray, he does note that on his first international game with Italy, 'I recall looking up to the sky. It was almost a prayer that this will go well. I don't know if this was something subconscious or how it happened, or if it was instilled in me as it is in my blood and family genetics.'

For him, preparation for high level sport is the individual putting in one hundred percent effort. 'Honest preparations lead to honest performances. I didn't put God into this. It was me and hard work.' He does acknowledge while in school, 'praying that no one would get seriously injured. I don't consider myself a religious person but when you get to key moments you turn to something.'

Ireland to Italy

Despite his circumstances, Ian knew in his heart that rugby was something he was good at, but he recalls a heart-to-heart discussion with his dad about whether he should retire aged 21 or not. 'He got me to put down the positives and negatives... and I eventually decided to stop.'

'Deep in my heart and head I just wanted to go back and play, but he got me to write a list of positives and negatives.' As part of his recovery, Ian returned to playing football with Kilmacud. This helped him reconnect with ball handling and being able to play and retrain his mind and his co-ordination. In time, these skills helped with his return to rugby with the Italian side Zebre.

Guiding Others with Vision Difficulty

THOUSANDS OF YOUNG rugby players around the world now wear the goggles that McKinley helped pioneer, and he is contacted regularly by partially sighted people who still want to succeed in sport.

'I get messages weekly from people who have had similar injuries or problems to mine. That's incredible. And knowing that 2,000 people around the world are using rugby goggles is wonderful. The idea of the goggles were in the pipeline but my brother Phillip put me in touch with an Irish design student, Johnny Merrigan, who is a very important part of this story. Myself, Phillip and Johnny got together and basically pushed the product over the line.'

Ian has not received any monetary reward for the goggles. 'I think being educated on the matter counts most. Like Covid-19, not many people knew about it. Now everyone seems to have read up on it.'

•••

Ian was offered a job coaching under-16s in Italy with a club called Leonoso. Even though he spoke no Italian he knew he needed a new start. It was a perfect arrangement. He needed to be somewhere where he was unknown. Being in the north of Italy helped him rediscover his passion for sport. His brother encouraged him greatly at this time. He came to realise that he could still work with a ball, the only problem was that he had no sight in one eye. The rugby community in Italy is small. Protecting his good eye would become a priority. Gouging of the eye is part of rugby and whilst illegal, it still happens. Even with only one eye, Ian noted that he still had attempts by opposing players to damage his good eye.

'I was gouged twice in my other eye. This was one of the reasons I stopped playing... and went down the path of getting eye protection.'

He discovered a company in Bologna that manufactured goggles that could help him protect his eye and play. It was clear to Ian that if he was to play rugby again, he would need protection.

With his new goggles, he needed to get approval from the various governing bodies. Italy was the first union to sign up to the goggles. In time, this would lead to a professional contract and also an International cap... playing for Italy! All the various unions were approached, however Ireland, England and France did not give approval, citing medical and insurance reasons. He persisted with his plans and backed up with research he was able to show the unions that they were wrong. It came to a head when his Italian club Zebre were due to play Connaught. Ian wrote to the Irish Rugby Union and informed them that he would be playing and wearing the goggles. In their reply, they noted that he could play, but not wear the goggles. He then started a campaign to overrule this position. A total of 13,000 people signed up to ask the IRFU to reverse their opinion. He met with the IRFU medical board to put forward his case. After a few days, they reversed their position.

'I played for Leinster and with Ireland under-20s. The rule is, if you represent your country, you can't change country. In 2017, after playing in Italy for three years, I became eligible to play for Italy.

'Playing for Italy as an Irish person is the proudest thing in my career. I have played against Ireland three times. It is hard to put into words what this means. Italy was the country that believed in me.

Reflecting on his career in rugby he acknowledges, 'I have played with some remarkable people in my career. However, I don't want sympathy. I wanted to win.

I had a chip on my shoulder and had a point to prove.'

Ian's self-belief got him through adversity. Many of his fellow players in Italy came from different countries and have quite different ways of preparing before a game. Whilst some of them prayed together, Ian did not join them. He believed that his game would be based on his ability and determination.

In 2021, he returned to Ireland and retired from playing. Living in Derry, where his wife Cordelia grew up, he focuses on family he is still connected with the game. Looking forward to putting his family first he intends to be remembered for that and not just a rugby career which was resurrected and overcame astonishing odds.

●●●

A documentary film about Ian's journey, entitled 'Look Beyond' was released in 2020 and features on Prime Video and Netflix.

'Talent is God given. Be humble. Fame is man-given. Be grateful. Conceit is self-given. Be careful.'

– John Wooden

Former US Basketball Coach and College Basketball Player

'In my faith I try to have more
balance both with my 'drive' and in
my spiritual life. Do we have 'zeal'
to become saints? To win the world
cup is the zeal of footballers. For
Christians it has to be to get to heaven!'

gerard hanley

FOOTBALLER

GER HANLEY WAS once described in an Irish newspaper as the... 'Holy Goalie' at Galway United. And he was a goalkeeper with serious talent, who toured with Ireland to the European under-17 Championships in 2008 but, as the paper hinted, the young man was also someone with a deep faith.

A well-known figure in the League of Ireland from his time at Mervue United, Dundalk, Shelbourne and Galway United, Ger would eventually give up on his love of football because he saw a greater role awaiting him in life.

He had done some work with various missionary and religious groups, but admits he was regularly torn between the two. Eventually, however, he left football behind and took on roles within faith-based groups. He currently works in the Archdiocese of Dublin.

From Galway, it was always his dream to be a professional football player. Ger came from a sporting family and GAA was part of the family life too. As a child he was involved in many sports... gaelic football, basketball, swimming... even a small bit of rugby. He tried everything. At 14, he decided to specialise in soccer rather that gaelic.

His first club was Knocknacarra FC and he played most of his underage football in the Salthill area. At 17, after four years with the club, he signed for Galway United.

Around this same time he had a chat with one of his coaches, Ken Kineane. 'He had a conversation with me and believed that I could make it. I learned from him. He was a strong early influence, and would have taken me aside at times to do a bit extra work on the pitch. I have had a lot of coaches over the years, but Ken's influence was crucial at this stage of my life' He also had other notable coaches, including Adrian Cronnan, Mark Colby and Tom Lally.

Drifting from Faith

'We always attended Mass as a family. I received all the sacraments. I was an altar server. However, gradually I became aware of it being less cool to be involved in Mass, or even going to Mass among my peers, many of whom had given up around the age of 11.

'I had taken Mass seriously as a server... but watching sport on TV I didn't think faith played a huge part in that part of our culture. Around this time, I too started to drift from faith but not consciously. By the time I went to secondary school I remember saying to someone, "I'd like to think God is real but he's probably not". It is a natural time for young people to question things, even if I was still being brought to church. However, the culture of sport drew me away from God. It just kind of happened.'

This is a natural experience for many teenagers. Peers are a huge influence on teenagers. 'Sport does a better job at keeping young people organised and involved. Sport will always be attractive. In church we don't offer Jesus as himself. If people don't connect with Jesus, they won't come back... and will find it boring and not alive. 'We need a renewal in the church. Our parishes are very uninspiring and not keeping us connected. My faith journey took place outside of the parish... and not in the parish. I didn't keep connected to the parish. I really didn't connect with God at this stage in my life. However, if you look at sport, it had a draw and appeal and felt like this was something worthwhile going after!'

Teammates

In Ger's experience there were not a lot of faith conversation or opportunities within the game. He recalled one teammate at Dundalk who was from Brazil and was an evangelical Christian. He read his bible daily and spoke openly about his faith. And he recalls one moment whilst on Ireland international team duty, when rooming with a teammate, having a very preliminary experience of trying to pray with another sportsperson.

'I was around 17 and we actually prayed the rosary together at an away game in Turkey representing Ireland. There might have been others who prayed too, I just didn't notice them. There were some elements of faith too. However, at this stage I didn't really know how to pray the rosary! It was an attempt to pray.'

Passion for the Premier League

Ger's big dream was to play in the Premier League in England and represent Ireland. This was a natural ambition, as he had played for Ireland since he was around 15 until 19. He played in European Championships, had trials in England, and he certainly was in the mix with people who were getting big offers in the UK. There was a chance. It was all about luck and time. He tried out with Ipswich Aberdeen, Plymouth, St Johnston… all around the same time.

'My passion for sport comes from me and my character. I like to give one hundred percent and also, I like to do things right. When it came to sport, it was about doing things right. Being disciplined and driven is important. I don't do things in halves… I like to do everything right. It wasn't just a love for soccer, but the effort of making it a success.'

Aberdeen did offer him a contract when he was 16. He points out that he didn't accept it as he wanted to go to England… not Scotland! Nothing personal! It was a very focused decision for someone so young. Ger was being led by his heart.

A Life without God

'I was setting myself up for a life without God. I hadn't seen, heard or experienced anything in my life up until then that would lead me to believe otherwise.'

For Ger, the big change happened when he was influenced by a teacher in school who was not afraid to talk about Jesus or matters of faith openly in the classroom. Some dismissed him. Ger was attracted to what he had to say. The same teacher organised retreats to Clonfert and to Knock Shrine. One day he notes, 'I remember a woman sharing her story of faith… then having an invitation to go to confession and attending Mass… and an encounter with Jesus in the Eucharist. This was the changing moment for me. The confession wasn't remarkable, but I just remember experiencing a sense of peace.

'Also, the priest brought the Blessed Sacrament in for a blessing (this is a Catholic thing!) and I remember an experience of God's presence … his loving presence. I knew Jesus was present then at that moment. I find it hard still to put words to this experience.'

It took time for Ger to process what had happened. and what was going on and changing within him. A year later, he had a similar experience on another retreat. These two episodes and encountering God confirmed to him that God is real. All this happened when he was just 14, a remarkable moment in anyone's life.

In his own words he notes, 'My conversion experience happened when I was that young. My faith was beginning to play a role in my life, asking questions like… *What does God want me to do? What role will God have in my life?* It was an increasing influence in my life at this time.

'I remember when I was in Ipswich walking through a park after training and, suddenly, I hoped that they would not offer me a contract as I was unsure at this time if this was something that I really wanted. I don't know why I felt this. Sport isn't always as glamorous as you think. It's a lot of hard work, especially at the level I was at. I was not a superstar or the next Ronaldo or Messi. I was striving just to make it. Going over as a teenager, there are all the temptations… and issues of loneliness. So in regards to my faith, I became more morally sensitive. There was lots of temptation that I would have to face on my own.'

The dream changed, but it was a long and slow process. His perspective was changing too. As he grew in faith, Ger slowly came to a realisation that having a career in football was not everything.

His big question was what God was asking him to do in his life. He dwelled on the question of where he was being *called*. He began to get involved in some local faith and prayer groups through his parish and in the area.

He was part of the Ark Prayer group in Galway and enjoyed the way they prayed, even if people were slightly older than him. He also worked for a year with the Youth 2000 retreat group, a Catholic youth movement for young people focused on prayer. Then he worked with *An Tobar Nua* in Galway around the time he signed for

Galway Utd. It is a café which serves as part of the Foundation in Christ Ministries, an ecumenical ministry founded by Kelly and Susan Curry, a couple from Kentucky in the United States. They also have a bookstore and a retreat group.

Ger was at a crossroads in his life, and a tension emerged in his sporting dream. He also noted a tension in living and expressing his faith while his peers experimented with other choices in life. He felt a growing tension in how to act morally. 'I became aware of my 'sin' and how to be free from it.' Up until then, his ambition in life was to be a footballer.

'Then I began to hear things, like God has a plan for you or the Holy Spirit will guide you... then 'Not my will, but your will'. It was scary to invite God in as the fear was that maybe God might ask me to leave football behind and do something else!'

As he noted, many of his friends didn't speak about faith as there was no context or space for that. It was a non-issue for them. 'We were all from very light faith communities. For the most part I hid my faith as I was scared what people would think of me.

'However, when I reached around 18 or 19 this changed. I started to get more connected with some Christian communities and started to talk to people about my faith. I joined a prayer group and had community support from other believers. I also started to pray in a new intentional way. Around this time, I prayed to receive the Holy Spirit and to have the courage to speak openly about my faith and witness to it also.'

Prayer began to become a bigger part of his life. He admired St Paul when he referred to self-control and athletes. 'The discipline of life as a footballer is crucial. I had injuries so I had to look after myself. I was disciplined around sleep, diet, gym work, exercise and so on. There is a great order in your day. I was able to merge this discipline from sport into my life of prayer. It started simply by getting up 10 minutes earlier every morning and create new habits of prayer, reading the bible... I started with Luke's Gospel, then tried to talk to God... and praying for my family.'

His football career was in peril because of injuries, and also Ger was moving clubs repeatedly, signing for Galway, Mervue, Dundalk and Shelbourne in a space of a few years. He had lots of disruption as he spent seven years in the League of Ireland between the ages of 17 and 24.

Making the Line

SINCE leaving football in January 2016, Ger has worked with NET Ministries, a group of young evangelical Catholic missionaries, for two years and then took on the position of Youth and Young Adult Ministry Coordinator at the Emmaus Centre, in Swords, leading a team which facilitates retreats for primary and secondary school students.

His life was turned upside down through an encounter with God on a school retreat and it is his privilege to be leading them for others now. 'For the last two years I have worked with the Archdiocese of Dublin and now I work with Alpha Ireland. I just want to be able to help to bring the message of faith to young people.'

God has a plan, and he firmly believes in that. Whilst not playing football anymore, he still enjoys sport. For him his Epitaph is *Servia* meaning... I will serve.

•••

He was always inspired by other footballers, such as goalkeepers Kasper Schmeichel and Shay Given. He not only wanted to be them, but to replace them. He just wanted to be the best. He also admires Roy Keane and his drive for perfections, and Paul McGrath who has had personal battles to overcome. Jurgen Klopp, the manager of Liverpool who openly speaks about being inspired by Jesus, is definitely someone Ger sees as a magnificent leader in life.

'In my faith, I try to have more balance both with my 'drive' and in my spiritual life. Do we have 'zeal' to become saints. To win the world cup is the zeal of footballers. For Christians it has to be to get to heaven!'

Choices must be made too, he acknowledges. 'I note the word sacrifice as one of being self-determined. The notion of sacrifice in sport is part of my journey away from football.'

Moving Away from Football

He did consider if his life was being drawn towards priesthood. He felt he needed to look at this question, and whilst in college in Galway he picked up a DVD on vocation to the priesthood but didn't think much about it. Around this time, he met Katie, now his wife.

He ended up going on a pilgrimage to Medjugorje in Bosnia and Herzegovina and bringing two questions for God! *Should he stay in football or become a priest… or none of the above?* 'I decided not to look for signs. At the end of the pilgrimage, I met three people and in conversation they noted that not only do we need priests, we also need good families and Catholic parents, and we need to hear about this vocation of marriage. I experienced the Holy Spirit speaking to me profoundly in this conversation. It was a new sense of joy that I was not called to priesthood.' Gradually his relationship grew and deepened.

'I met my now wife at 19. I reflected that if I am driven in football, I cannot give myself, and time, to her as my career develops. I remember listening to Paul O'Connell speaking of sacrifice. He noted his wife made the greatest sacrifice, not him, while he was playing for Munster and Ireland. I sacrificed my pure dedication to football to spend more time with her. I rebalanced my time spent with her over time with football.' Choices have to be made, he agrees, on the life and balance of relationships and sport. He chose his wife over football.

'On one level, you have to get real. To be honest, I didn't have a particularly amazing career in the League of Ireland. I had a few good moments. Apart from that, I had a lot of injuries, a lot of setbacks. I could have kept going and pushed on and given everything and left the youth work and ministry aside. In my heart, what I feel is more important is that young people come to know God.

'I have shared my faith story often with people. Sport is good. However, it won't fully satisfy in a way that God will satisfy. I've tried both and experienced both. People who have been in both worlds have an opportunity. For me, I value my faith more than I did playing for Ireland! That doesn't mean playing for Ireland wasn't great. It just doesn't come out on top for me. You can't blame young people for not being part of faith.

In hindsight, he notes that he followed his football dream for 12 years. He has no regrets, but acknowledges he gave his best. As he looks behind him and also into the future, Ger is convinced that God was guiding and leading him into a deeper relationship. 'My life is not one I choose. I was called to live my life as it is today. I wanted football, but God had a different plan.'

●●●

'Sports is the best means of communication between people from different religions and countries.'

— Yao Ming

Chinese Basketball Executive and Former Professional Player

'Yes, I have thanked God for my success
and all my involvement in cycling. If I
stayed here I would not have had those
opportunities. In a way, my life was
blessed because of cycling.'

seán kelly

CYCLIST

HE WAS BAPTISED John James after his father and then, in the Irish tradition to avoid confusion, he was called Seán, the Irish form of John. There only could be one Seán Kelly. And before him, there was only one Irish cyclist on the tip of everyone's tongues… Shay Elliott.

Elliott was the first Irishman to make a career as a professional bike rider. He was the first to ride in the Tour de France. First to win a stage, and first to wear the yellow jersey.

Growing up on the family farm in Curraghduff in Waterford, Seán Kelly won the famed Shay Elliott Memorial race two months shy of his 18th birthday. He successfully defended his title the following year, and he was on his way… chasing the legend of Elliott. There were race wins as an amateur all over these islands. He won on the continent too. And, in December 1976, the legend of Seán Kelly itself more formally commenced.

A private plane landed in Ireland and the men on board headed south, Jean de Gribaldy amongst them. In the Kelly household, they were told Seán was not at home. They went to look for him and found him… coming down the road on a tractor.

Yes, the legend of Seán Kelly begins with the cycling king on an old tractor.

In January 1977, he was a professional cyclist, living over the bike shop run by de Gribaldy, and competing for the Frenchman and the Flandria team. In the next 17 years, until his retirement in 1994, he won 193 races in total. Nine were the Monument Classics, the oldest and toughest one-day races in the world. He won the famous Paris-Nice race seven years in-a-row. He won one of the great Tours, the 1988 Vuelta a España. He won four green jerseys in the Tour de France. For five years, he was number one in the world rankings.

On Kelly's tail, quickly would come Stephen Roche and others. The trail forged by Elliott all those years before, now had Irishmen ambitiously fighting one another for glory and taking on the best of the best in the world.

'It is disappointing to recall that when we were flying the Irish flag all over the world, we got very little recognition for our efforts in the early years. It wasn't until we started winning that people began to take an interest. In those early days it is hard to believe... but we were winning everything!' explains Seán.

Learning to Work Hard

Along with his brother Joe, Seán attended the local primary school in Crehana, in Waterford. He is remembered by his fellow classmates as being very quiet, a quietness that became a characteristic of Seán's as he grew older. His formal education ended when he was 13, when he left school to work on the family farm. At 16 he also worked as a bricklayer.

'Being raised on a farm, we had to do a lot of tough work. You learn how to work hard and stay committed on a daily basis. This helped in other aspects of my life.'

A family faith would also help.

'My mother and dad were devoted church-goers in the local parish of Clonea. I would have grown up in that environment. Going to Mass at the weekend was normal for us at home. I have fond memories of attending the local parish Stations.... going from house to house and meeting neighbours. There were prayers said in the neighbours' houses.'

Similar to nearly all young sports enthusiasts, it was difficult to combine a regular attendance at church and the scheduling of competitions.

'I was a regular mass-goer until I went to France. I lost contact with that part of my life as many of the races and events were held over the weekends. In my early days cycling I certainly had a miraculous medal. My mother would have given it to me when I was going away travelling.'

Seán's first race was held at Kennedy Terrace in Carrickbeg. He won it! At the age of 16 he had won the national junior championship. He had a senior licence before he was 18 and soon became a winning cyclist at home.

'It was a dream to go to France as a young cyclist. As a junior under-18 we went abroad to events in the UK, France and the World Championships in Germany. I got a taste of serious cycling.'

Regrets... He has a Few

One of the regrets he has is the misjudgement he made in 1976 as he prepared for the Olympics in Montreal. He travelled to South Africa to ride the Rapport Tour in preparation also for the Olympics, at a time when there was an international ban on athletes competing in South Africa. Racing under a pseudo name he was identified by a journalist who was covering a socialite wedding.

'I do have regrets. Such as the races you didn't win. I didn't win the World Championships. Now my career is over, there are regrets for races I just missed out on. Then there is the Olympics. I went to South Africa in my early days and I got suspended. I was banned from going to the Olympics. If I had gone to the Olympics I will never know what I could have achieved over the years. You just never know what plan is laid out for you.'

As he settled into the hard life of a professional cyclist, Seán remained one of the quiet ones, saying little. 'There were people in the team, and we would talk about so many things, including our beliefs. Some of the Spanish and French lads were regular church-goers. You would talk about that in some ways, but not going into too much detail. I wouldn't ask too many personal questions.'

He also notes that, 'in France in my later career, particularly before the large races, I would say a prayer to keep me safe and to do my best... and not to have any bad luck. This was just something I believed in.'

His personal prayer was just to give his all.

'It was to give my best. The Spanish riders, and also some of the French, would have blessed themselves at the start of a race. It was something I did myself. Now I wouldn't be praying on the bike... that was just pure focus. I would say

Seán Kelly Square

IN 1982, IN a tribute to his achievements on the World stage – in the Tour de France and elsewhere – Carrick-in-Suir named its town square in honour of its brilliant 'son'.

'For me Seán is a rider who has invisible buttons on his handlebars,' Ireland's Stephen Roche once explained. 'There is one which says "fast" and another which says "slow". When he is going well all he has to do is touch those buttons and the response is immediate.'

Roche, who would claim a famous Tour de France title in 1987, also further explained Kelly's impact on him as a younger cyclist. 'Seán Kelly was a pro, but he came from Carrick-on-Suir. He'd have nails for breakfast. I'm a Dubliner from the city. How am I gonna compete with all these guys?'.

•••

something privately to myself at the start. I suppose it was a prayer of sorts.'

He does recall that there was no real religious culture on the various teams he cycled with. Yet on one occasion, whilst he was wearing the green jersey in the Tour de France, the team were staying near Lourdes. 'The people that I lived with were from Belgium… and they took the bouquet that I was presented with and placed it in the Shrine in Lourdes.'

His wife Linda once was spotted putting something into her husband's jersey at the start of one of the Classics (Liege-Bastogne). She revealed it was just a sprig of blessed palm. 'Every Palm Sunday, I give him a bit if he is racing, it can't do any harm,' she explained.

In August 1991 while Seán was competing the Tour of Galicia, his brother Joe was killed in a race near Carrick-on-Suir. This deeply impacted on Seán. He notes that one of the ways he honours his brother's memory was 'to continue to do well for him'. He did. He went on to win many more races. He dedicated his win in Lombardy later in the year to his brother.

Seán Kelly may not have won the Tour de France, but he did win the hearts of cycling enthusiasts in Ireland and overseas. He was able to go shoulder-to-shoulder with the greatest. He also was the best on so many occasions. He retired from cycling in 1994 and returned to live and farm in Ireland with his wife Linda Grant, daughter of Dan Grant who mentored Seán in his early days of cycling.

For Seán, as he looks back, he recalls the mentoring of some of the people in Carrick-on-Suir such as Tony Ryan and Dan. 'What is important for me is that these men took an interest in us in our youth.'

'When I retired it was not easy after 18 years to just give it up. Suddenly… it all finishes. You have to find things to do. Your training and competing change in retirement. It takes a few years to adapt. You can be financially secure but adjustment is not an easy path.

'When I got out of cycling, I got away from it. For the first couple of years I didn't go to races at all. I needed that time to clear my head.'

The Voice of Cycling

He has become one of the voices of cycling commentary. In 2006, he launched Ireland's first professional cycling team, the Seán Kelly Team.

'Cycling is still a minority sport here in Ireland. We have the talent. We just need the correct resources going into it to nurture and develop it.' Looking to the future, he notes, 'We have Sam Bennett, but also Nico Roche, Dan Martin over the years doing well. This is special because Sam comes from my home town of Carrick.'

He continues to cycle for leisure and supports various charities. 'I still cycle, depending on my schedule. I like to keep fit and get on the bike, and even do a few charity cycles. I still enjoy it. I still feel good after a cycle! Just do what you are able to do is the motto now.'

Seán is grateful for everything he has achieved. 'When I sit back and reflect on my career... the wins, losses... an amazing career of opportunities... to travel and meet so many people. Learning new languages. All of these things. I say to myself, *My God wasn't I lucky to get involved in cycling and all the good things that I received from it.* In his own way, he notes he is still religious and spiritual, something that has evolved as he has aged.

Seán Kelly is clearly one of the greatest cyclists of his generation. He went on to make peace with the fact that even the greatest cyclists may never win the greatest race... the Tour de France.

'Yes, I have thanked God for my success and all my involvement in cycling. If I stayed here I would not have had those opportunities. In a way, my life was blessed because of cycling.'

For Seán, he would like to be remembered as someone who was a hard worker and 'always gave my best.' Simply... Quietly.

●●●

'Sports teaches you character, it teaches you to play by the rules, it teaches you to know what it feels like to win and lose – it teaches you about life'

– Billie Jean King

American Former World No 1 Tennis Player

ANOTHER calling

'I don't have it all worked out, but my belief is unique to me and maybe not the same as everyone else. I believe we have the ability to do wonderful things during our time on earth.'

tracy piggot

BROADCASTER

TRACY PIGGOTT IS racing royalty. Born in England but now based in Kildare, she is the daughter of Susan Armstrong and the legendary Lester Piggott, who died in May of 2022. Her dad, who famously rode Shergar to a Derby victory in 1981, died in Switzerland at 86 years of age. Writing on her Instagram page, Tracy said, 'It's a sad, sad day. Daddy, I will miss you so much'. She accompanied the post with a picture of her father, who was one of the greatest flat jockeys of all time.

A month before Lester's passing, Tracy and her daughter Thea unveiled a statue of him at the Guineas Festival at the Curragh, where he had previously clocked up five Derby victories. In total, Lester won 30 British Classic races in a career which yielded 4,493 winners, alongside 116 Royal Ascot victories. He was named champion jockey 11 times between 1960 and '82.

Tracy's royal racing lineage goes much further back, however. Her great-grandfather Ernest Piggott won the Grand National as a jockey three times, in 1912, '18 and '19, while her grandfather Keith Piggott won the Grand National as a trainer in 1963. She can trace her horsing pedigree back to the 1600's on her dad's side to her Quaker roots and the Day family.

Her early years were spent in Cambridge and Newmarket in south-east England, where she was surrounded by the whole horse culture. She began to move from the passive pony riding to riding out horses from when she was aged around 11. Tracy has retained huge love and connection with animals since her childhood, as she notes, 'I have always been connected to animals'.

After her school years, she worked as a 'galloper' or exercise rider in the U.S. before settling in Ireland in 1986. 'I never really knew or had a plan for what I wanted to do after school... but I knew I wanted to travel, so I ended up in the US for four years. I had planned to be my dad's assistant, but that changed.' Lester was convicted of tax evasion and ended up serving time (13 months) in prison.

As a result of this the family plans changed. Her mother Susan took over the training licence. Her mum's dad was Sam Armstrong, a well-known UK trainer, who coincidently had a horse yard in the Curragh, in Kildare, before the Second World War. In time, Tracy would end up in Co Kildare, close to the Curragh. Her grandfather was closely connected to Vincent O'Brien, one of Ireland's greatest horse trainers. During the 1950s she notes that they were 'trail blazers', seeking excellence in breeding lines and visiting and buying horses in the US.

After her time in the States she then became part of her mum's equine insurance business. 'She had the eye for a winner and pedigree. She had an amazing eye for a horse, she was a very successful bloodstock agent and went onto becoming a very successful horse trainer... she was so good at what she did.' Her mum's business partner was Cormac McCormick. 'They were successful against the odds in the bloodstock industry. Working with them helped me to travel and visit many countries, and also to be involved with Goffs in Kildare and Tattersalls in Newmarket and Meath, where I developed a huge affinity with Ireland.'

First of all, she moved to New Ross in Wexford to a stud farm. This was a quieter place as opposed to a racing stable. From there, she moved to Golden in Tipperary and worked as an assistant to horse trainer and winning Grand National jockey Tommy Stack, who was well known for his association with Red Rum. It was during that time that she rode a winner at Leopardstown in 1988.

'I only rode in a few races, even though when I was younger I had wanted to be a jockey... but I soon realised it was not for me.'

Tracy continues to ride out horses, training and exercising them daily.

Stories of Faith

Tracy comes from a family that were traditionally rooted in the Church of

England. She recalls special memories as a child of seeing her parents kneeling at the side of their bed praying, though not really church-goers in a traditional sense. Tracy went to boarding school in Ely on the Fens.

'I was good at scripture in primary school and always fascinated by the stories of the Gospels... Jesus and the stories of faith.' She also recalls her daily school assemblies that took place in the world famous and stunning Ely Cathedral. 'We didn't appreciate it at the time. It was only later in life that I appreciated the beauty of the building and how privileged we were to be there each morning... there in all its glory.' Looking back on her faith now Tracy is thankful for the religious values that she inherited and tries to live by. 'I have a strong faith, but it is more unique to me. I know there is a creator... a presence.

'Is it God? Probably, yes. God is probably the word I was brought up with. God can be many things to different people. However, I do talk with friends about God. I don't have it all worked out, but my belief is unique to me and maybe not the same as everyone else. I believe we have the ability to do wonderful things during our time on earth. Some do, and some do not and go in the other direction.

'Wonderful things can be as simple as putting out a hand to help someone in need to cross the road, or pick up something they have dropped... to saving lives, each act is hugely meaningful and can make great change. Right now, it's about trying to preserve our beautiful planet. We were given this amazing place to live, and now we are reaping the effects of not looking after what we were given.'

She recalls that in 1988, shortly before she won her race in Leopardstown, her mum had a serious accident with a horse and ended up in hospital for six weeks. It was a traumatic time as this was also the period her dad was in prison. 'I did pray to God to help her pull through. I have always felt that presence.'

Tracy acknowledges that her beliefs have evolved as she has matured.

Life in Front of the Camera

In 1989, she began working as a broadcaster with RTE. This came after a chance encounter with Johnathon Irwin, who ran the Phoenix Park Racecourse. A seed was planted. Later, Tim O'Connor, former Head of RTÉ sport, would invite her to take on a role with the national broadcaster. It was in the mid-90s that she started presenting the flagship sports programme *Sports Stadium* for seven

Stunned Just Once in her RTE Career

TRACY WORKED AT racecourses for over 30 years with RTE and resonated with viewers because of her wit and charm. Only once was she left virtually speechless, when in the company of trainer Peter Casey, who had just enjoyed a victory with Flemenstar at Leopardstown.

'He was a delight to interview, but in a precarious way because you never knew what he would come out with. He always had a glint in his eye like a mischievous schoolboy,' Tracy explained later. 'There was something that shone out of him. A real genuineness and likability, so when he started getting big wins with Flemenstar I was so delighted for him.

'I was always aware he could say anything, but I never thought he would say what he said that day at Leopardstown.' Casey told viewers that he was so happy he was going to end his day with sex.

'I remember what happened as if it was yesterday. It had been pouring all day and I was wearing this ridiculous hat that I had to keep draining of rainwater.'

•••

years, whilst also concentrating on horse racing presentation. She anchored the coverage for four Olympic Games, the Special Olympics and the Paralympics, and has been a pitch-side reporter for rugby internationals and Heineken Cup matches for eight seasons. 'I loved it immensely,' she stresses.

She loved bringing out the best in people, 'I was good at it and enjoyed making people feel comfortable. You find out a lot about people when interviewing them. My job was to bring the best out of people. I would adjust my approach depending on who it was I was interviewing.' Tracy went on to work on other television programmes, assisting in the production of the documentary *The Young Prince of Ballydoyle*, and anchoring the sports quiz series, *At the End of the Day*. She hosted the RTE Sport Awards for several years. In 2008, she appeared on *The Restaurant*, while in 2013 she was a contestant on *Celebrity MasterChef Ireland*.

For Tracy, family is a priority. She admires people who make a difference. Her daughter's godfather is a priest with the Pallottine order, Father Mike O'Sullivan. She admires how people like him can devote their life to living the Gospel and putting it into action in a real way for people. She admires people who have a strong faith and are comfortable about doing it in public ways, but for Tracy her faith is private and personal. She has an admiration for Pope Francis and the change he is trying to be in the world. Life for Tracy now is lived at a slower pace. She still has her passion for horses still has dreams to fulfil. Whilst acknowledging that she has some regrets in life, she still wants to make a difference. 'I want to give something back… I have had mostly a very fulfilled life.'

Reflecting on where she is today, she is deeply thankful for the blessings she has received in life. 'I give thanks to God all the time …every day! We are so blessed to live in a beautiful country. My pleasure is walking with my dogs… I just love the enthusiasm of them. These are things I can appreciate. 'As I slow down and get a bit older, I am very much connected to creation. I try not to be materialistic. When you strip it back, it is the basic simple things in life that matter.'

Tracy would like to be remembered as someone who 'cared' about the important things in life. God is part of her life in a guiding way. She likes to acknowledge His presence… in the words of Garth Brooks, *'Some of God's greatest gifts are unanswered prayers!'*

●●●

'I have taken God to task a few
times… questioned what happened.
Ultimately, however, I still trust in God
and know he has a plan for me.'

olive foley

MOTHER AND WIFE

LOSING HER HUSBAND, the legendary Munster and Ireland rugby player Anthony Foley, so early in life meant that Olive Foley experienced her grief in a public manner. The man they fondly called 'Axel' was coach of Munster when he died from acute pulmonary oedema on a club trip to Paris, on October 16, 2016, in advance of a Champions League game against Racing 92. He was just 42 years of age. A mother to two children, Tony and Dan, who were 11 and eight when their dad died, Olive felt the love and sympathy of the whole sporting community in the island of Ireland, and beyond, but she was also left with a huge void in her life.

Olive and her children had lost a loving husband and father.

The Irish rugby community had lost one of the most cherished of individuals too. Anthony had made his debut for Ireland in 1995, in the Five Nations Championship, when he scored against England. He would play over 60 times for his country and represent Ireland in two World Cup finals. For Munster, the legendary figure of Anthony Foley was even bigger… he played over 200 times in the famed red jersey, and led Munster to European victory in 2006.

A Banking Career

Olive is from a village Dromgrainey near Scariff. Her mother was a primary school teacher, and her dad was a farmer and butcher. After boarding with the Presentation Sisters in Thurles, and college, she worked in the banking sector and travelled extensively around the country.

'The Foley's and my family were well known to each other,' Olive explains. 'When I was in boarding school in Thurles, Anthony's sister Orla attended also. We shared lifts to and from school, so from an early age I was familiar with Anthony. We didn't start going out for quite a while later... I was 22 when we started going out.' Her family were quite traditional church-goers.

'I remember going to morning Mass with my mother as a child. I still go to morning Mass to this day, when possible. The quiet church is a treasured memory. I remember on one visit to the church, we were in the gallery, and I heard the priest talk about the children of Medjugorje whom Our Lady appeared to.

'I was so struck that our Lady had appeared to children. I remember at the time being very taken by this information. Later in my twenties, I decided to go there on pilgrimage. I was married at the time. I phoned home to Anthony, and he was wondering what I was doing. I told him I was at Mass, said the rosary... adoration and more prayers.

'I laugh now at his response... "Olive did you really sign up for all that!"

For Olive, her faith is deeply important to her. Like every relationship it may not be on the same level for every couple. However, she notes that Anthony never judged her faith commitment and was very supportive of her bringing their young children to Mass and other ceremonies.

'I always believed that Anthony had great faith. He was a deep thinker. He may not have expressed his faith in a traditional manner... but he was not against expressing faith either. He would have had a traditional Catholic upbringing, like many of us. However, like many of his generation playing sport, this took on a greater role and his commitment to practicing his faith lessened.' Something that is not uncommon among those involved in elite sport.

It is not easy bringing up teenagers, as many peers drop out of the regular practice of faith. Olive does point out that she tries to instil in her children the importance of daily prayer, even if it is the last few thoughts in the day.

'Recently we attended Mass as a family on Anthony's anniversary. I was quite taken by how much they participated in the responses. Very few who go to Mass rarely say they don't like it… for me, going to Mass gives me peace and a little bit of joy!'

The Stars Align

Anthony and Olive began to 'go out with one another' after being set up by family members in January 1999 at a rugby match in Cork.

'By all accounts, Anthony had his eye on me. I was brought to Cork shopping with Anthony's sister Orla and his mother. I was then brought to Temple Hill to watch a game. It was my first rugby match… as I had never been!' In Anthony's words, "All I remember was being smitten from the start".'

Olive was not big into sports and was more interested in Irish dancing, plays and the arts. Clearly differences attract! After the post-match festivities, Olive returned to Limerick on the Munster team bus. For Anthony, he had discovered the right person to help him balance his life in new ways. Around this time, Anthony was playing for Munster and Ireland, and the game was all consuming for him. 'Rugby went from zero in my life to almost one hundred percent everything that I was doing,' Olive also explains. 'I was going to matches… there was the social life. All of his life was rugby and I got to know some really good people.' At the time of Anthony's death, Olive recalls the role that her faith played for her.

'When I get up in the morning I pray, and give thanks for being alive. I say a Hail Mary. This is something that I have always done. Giving thanks for everything is important to me. God is part of my life every day… throughout the day. I have great faith in God. 'At the time of Anthony's death, I recall saying, This is the path that is for us. This was God's plan, and we must trust in his plan.

'I get peace from this. Also, our lives are short… our journey of life is going towards eternity. Around Anthony's death I was struck by simple acts of prayer… and kindness people showed to me. Every Mass card I believe helped at that time. It helped me to know that Anthony was being carried in prayer into his new life.

'I firmly believe that I will join him again in heaven.'

A Discipline Instilled

Anthony Foley's dad Brendan had played rugby for Munster and Ireland and was part of the team that famously beat the All Blacks in 1978, 12-0 at Thomond Park. Anthony grew up in Killaloe and was involved in many sports, lining out locally for the parish in gaelic football and hurling.

His lifelong friend Keith Wood summed him up simply, 'Heart, honesty, determination... and a team player'. Anthony acknowledged in *Axel: A Memoir* that being a boarder in St Munchin's in Limerick gave him the discipline that would see him through life. The president of the school Fr Garry Bluett was a mentor to him and also became a life-long friend. Fr Garry also officiated at the wedding of Olive and Anthony in 1999.

Whilst in school, the routine of sport was also matched by the rituals of daily prayers morning and evening. 'The routine was definitely a good preparation for rugby,' he admitted in his memoir.

Rugby was everything to Anthony, but his family meant more. He was a dedicated dad and had no problem switching between rugby and being dad. He enjoyed his playing career and had few regrets at the end of it.

Olive has reflected often on the loss that she has experienced. The sudden death of her husband made headlines around the world and not just in the family of rugby. She admits that she is still coming to terms daily on living with loss. 'Many people have experienced loss. Mine is no greater than others. But losing Anthony with no notice... my husband, my confidant... my best friend, but perhaps most of all the father of my children. It created a void that's impossible to fill.

'Having family has helped to deal with the pain. I have a great family, my immediate family, Anthony's family... my family of friends, my family of faith, and my family of church. All of these are essential to us.'

She describes the early hours after being informed of his death. 'In those darkest hours, the arms of that family wrapped their arms me and my family in a way that was remarkable... and have done so ever since.'

In the days after Axel's death, her sons also had to come to terms with their massive loss. Tony, one of the boys, came up with the idea of getting people to honour his dad by going to Mass.

'Tony had been busy thinking of a tribute to his dad and asked that a Facebook page be set up in his memory. He wants to use it to ask people, who want to show their support, to attend Mass on each of the next eight Sundays to pray for people who have died and, while there, to offer a prayer for his dad also.'

Anthony Foley was a big man with No 8 on his back most often. His teammates, subsequently, stood in mourning on the pitch in the figure of eight. The jersey with that number was retired for a period also as a mark of respect.

Now, for his son to also relate to that number was significant.

'Tony asked everyone if you would, in his dad's memory, like and share this page. As you do that, tag eight Facebook friends to go to Mass over the next eight Sundays and, at that Mass, light a candle for a loved one. It was such a lovely idea.'

This idea captured the imagination of many not just in Limerick, but also further afield and outside of Ireland.

Family of Sport

Olive also pointed out that November is a special time in Ireland for remembering those who have died. Traditionally in Ireland, people would pray for the dead in November and for the 'Holy Souls'.

'The eight Sundays will take us right up to Christmas, which is a special family time, of course, but can be very difficult for families who have lost loved ones.

'Anthony was an idol to many, without a shadow of doubt, but it was at home where he was idolised the most. He was very close to the children, and they were his priority. We were number one. I'm afraid to say, rugby came a close second... he was a great family man.' Olive has never stepped back from Anthony's former giant presence in the rugby community. 'I can divide my sporting world of friends into three distinct groups,' she admits. 'There is Shannon... the Munster folk... and the Ireland gang. The team from Shannon is very close to me. The players keep in touch with me, as do their wives. We are still very close. 'They prop me up and keep me on track. The Munster group... Anthony played the longest with this group. I have stayed in touch with many of them. Many keep calling and looking out for me. Now my sons are getting messages from some of the former players.

'Anthony would be delighted that the teams are looking out for his sons.'

She remarks on the role of former Munster and Ireland coach, Declan Kidney around the time of Anthony's passing. 'Declan Kidney, to name one person, has been an immense support. His wife Anne died the Tuesday before Anthony died.

A Book for Life

NEW rituals for the Foley family became important after the sudden death of Anthony. Bedtime prayer took on a new form.

'We always say that Anthony's memoir is something that I'm very privileged to have. In the beginning we'd go to bed early at night and we'd say our prayers and then I'd read a few pages from his book.

'Their eyes would be wide open. They'd really enjoy this and then, inevitably, they'd have questions… and they'd just love it.'

●●●

The last time I saw Anthony was the day he went to Anne's funeral and then he went to Cork to fly to Paris. Declan was one of the visitors in the hours after Anthony's death. It is good to be able to talk to him about loss and bereavement.'

'I have taken God to task a few times… questioned what happened. Ultimately, however, I still trust in God and know he has a plan for me.'

Olive also notes the role of Sister Helen Culhane, founder of Limerick's Children Grief Centre, and admits that her family would have found it even more difficult to deal with death and grief without that support.

'I had never heard about it before Anthony's death. A local teacher pointed it out to me, as it might be helpful to my children who were grieving also. The centre and all the people there have transformed our lives. As a family we have been helped in our grief and have come to a new understanding of where we are in dealing with death and loss. I really clicked with Sr Helen on our first encounter. She is an amazing woman of faith. 'Talking about death became important for the whole family. It helped them come to terms with grief. So now I'm talking about dad to the children instead of, "let's pretend this never happened, don't mention dad because everybody's going to cry".'

Sr Helen and her team helped to create the space for the family to remember and connect with Anthony in a pastoral and healing way.

'Sr Helen helped us open up the conversation, so for the last 10 minutes I'm now talking quite freely to the children about Dad. Then we were able to continue the conversation on the way home in the car, and then next thing, we're talking about him morning, noon and night… because he comes up in conversation constantly.'

Olive is now an ambassador for the Grief Centre and helps with fundraising and creating an awareness of the work. 'I still have a deep connection to Anthony and reflect that he is still part of our lives.

'We are happy. My kids are great and give me purpose. They have had great support. We have great friends. I am lucky… thank God. I am full of peace and have no regrets in my life. Our family has lived every minute to the fullest.

'I believe God is very much part of my life every day. I am surrounded by good people, and I am very grateful to them. The first trauma in our lives was Anthony dying. I am grateful I had 17 great years with Anthony. Some people don't get that much.'

●●●

epilogue

Bishop Fintan Monahan (top) and (below) John Boyers, Mark Fleming,
Philip Mitchell and Martin Lewis.

Fintan Monahan
BISHOP

FINTAN MONAHAN IS one of Ireland's youngest and possibly fittest Bishops. He has a passion for his ministry and also loves being active.

Fintan grew up in Tullamore, in Offaly until his parents moved back to their native county Galway in 1980. His family set up in An Cheathrú Rua, where his father was principal at Scoil Chuimsitheach Chiaráin, and subsequently moved to his mother's native Castlegar in 1996.

At local comprehensive school in An Cheathrú Rua, he was introduced to a great number of sports, and began a life-long interest in basketball. On a slightly less active front, Fintan also found himself fishing in the lakes of Connemara during the summer.

In that part of Galway, the GAA was of course a dominant factor in the community. 'We had a good football team and we won the Connacht title in our senior year. Connemara is mainly a footballing area... we played lots of it, but I also played hurling at the weekend with Castlegar.

'I was always keen on golf too. I took that from my dad, who was a single handicap golfer. I used to go and play with him, and I played a lot of golf when I was on staff in St Jarlath's College. I haven't played so much since I moved to Ennis as Bishop. I have been occupied with other matters.' Running and cycling now challenge for Fintan's attention in his downtime!

'Where possible I cycle everywhere... it is so healthy, good for the environment, and it keeps me out of the car and heavy traffic!'

His parents ensured that traditional elements of faith at home were observed in a normal, 'fairly traditional' manner. 'They prayed personally and even at times in the car going on a journey there might be a rosary said on the way. Outside of Sunday Mass, we would go a little more frequently during Advent and Lent.' A huge influence in Fintan's young life was his grandfather.

'I also spent a lot of time with my grandfather. He was the caretaker in the church and general handy man. He also went to a lot of the devotions. The faith that was handed on to me was simple... it was one of no fuss. It was one influenced by prayer to Our Lady and attending Mass. It was based on reading the bible, religious literature that was available at home.'

'Fr Tommy Mannion, the local school chaplain, was a big influence on me too. He was huge into athletics and he brought us to all the events. He influenced a whole generation around my age.' Fintan began to find the priesthood an option for his life journey, because of how people like Tommy and his parents lived their faith.

But, he was within a great community of believers, including the local Presentation Sisters. 'I was surrounded by great believers and ordinary people of faith. I was also impressed by the hurlers of Castlegar and Galway, however... people like Joe Connelly and Iggy Clarke. They were the greatest hurlers in Ireland and they had a phenomenal faith, as did other lads from the teams.

'They were role models and involved in the practice of their faith. They were influential on the pitch but also in how they lived their life!'

In his late teens, Fintan, like around 60 others of his age, decided to pursue his vocation to the priesthood, in the national seminary in Maynooth.

'It was only when I went to Maynooth, where I got exposed to some amazing thinkers such as Thomas Merton, John Henry Newman, CS Lewis... did my faith really begin to deepen. I was also introduced to the writings of Joseph Ratzinger, intellectual giants like Thomas Aquinas and many other contemporary spiritual writers. My mind was expanding and my faith was deepening.

'In Maynooth, whilst studying science there was no time for anything, but when I studied theology most of my afternoons were free, so I was able to play racquetball, football, hurling and run... there was plenty of free time, and I used it to stay fit and healthy!'

He was ordained a priest for the Archdiocese of Tuam on June 16, 1991.

After ordination, he was a curate in An Tulach, Baile na hAbhann, between 1992 and '93, during which he completed a licentiate in biblical theology and a higher diploma in education from NUI Galway. Whilst he was there he played with a few football teams and both played and coached basketball in Inverin. After his post-grad he was appointed to staff in St Jarlath's College, Tuam, one of the blue blood GAA schools in the country!

'I was a fish out of water there as my background was hurling and basketball. It had a huge football ethos. They barely tolerated basketball! Despite that, I managed to coach and, eventually, I even coached a few teams that went on to win national competitions. I was there 23 years and had a happy and fulfilling association with sports in the school.'

It wasn't all sport. Boarders and staff were almost like a family.

'As boarders... you were a family. There was a strong connection with the lads, between school, eating, sport... and just normal life. Many students talked to me about their questions and struggles of faith.'

It was natural for the students to pray before a match, as there was an ethos of team prayer. 'The senior team would say a prayer... various priests over the years kept this tradition going. It was taken very seriously by all the teams, really... prayer was part and parcel of the build-up routine.'

In 2016, Fintan was chosen by Pope Francis to be Bishop of Killaloe in Clare.

'Within minutes of where I live, you are in the Burren and some of the most amazing countryside in Ireland.

'I never expected it. I really enjoyed what I was doing and was ready for a parish in Connemara. It was totally unexpected being appointed a bishop, never mind being a parish priest!'

Fintan is someone who has a passion for running for pleasure. 'I love getting outside and keeping my mind healthy. It is a oneness with nature. I am not a lover of long days spent inside. Even though that is a lot of my day as bishop. For me, being a bishop, running is a lifeline. I get to plan my day but try to do some fresh air exercise daily. It is hard to get out in the morning as I have Mass and prayers to say! I have more time later in the day between meetings.

'For me running is also sociable. I am part of a group that meets every Saturday morning. There could be up to 60 running and a few of us also meet up to run during the week, if time allows. Currently, I am running 10k around five times a week... at weekends I do more. From June that will increase as we focus on the Dublin Marathon.

'We will add 1k on to our weekly run building up for the marathon. So by the end, we will be up to 22 miles... around three weeks before the marathon. I have run around 20 marathons and double that figure for half-marathons. I am not fast but happy to just compete. I have never broken the three-hour barrier and at my age never will!'

As a student of science, he explains what happens to him as he runs.

'In my mind, there is a whole sequence... the preparation, the nerves, the awareness of the great challenge… during the marathon there is a mental energy trying to pace yourself and sticking to your goals. You hit the wall… you can see it coming. I face it with determination and strong will, and draw on inner reserves.

'You never lose the thrill of taking part. Even now as I am older, the thrill is still huge for me and my personal targets of achievement. You push yourself to the limit. And there's the satisfaction of finishing.

'Sometimes, in a run I might pray or get into saying the rosary. The Hail Mary's can keep me going. However, inevitably as you run, someone might be with you and chatting. Sometimes people are great to help you get through the challenges of the run.

'People talk to me during the runs about some of the personal challenges of life. Because they see me and can identify me, they feel free to talk to me and ask for advice. I see this as a privilege. It's the same as walking the Camino in Spain… almost everyone taking part has an interesting faith angle.

'You might drift with someone for a few days and get to know them in ways that would not happen if you were in a large group.

'I don't see it as a burden being identified as a bishop running. I take things very naturally. I am very happy to chat to people, but I am equally happy being on my own running for a few miles too. As I age, I can go slower and keep chatting!

'I remember on the long walks on the Camino, I would often find myself meditating… remembering prayers, thinking about parts of the scripture… thinking of key people in my life. I would find myself digging deep into what makes me tick.

'I find myself totally re-created when I return from the Camino. It is the same as a retreat, you return a little more 'whole' and different as a person. It is the release of endorphins associated with exercise too.

'I find on the Camino that I am happy… just getting up in the morning and walking… the freedom to just walk! I have completed the whole of the Camino over 20 days and I have brought many groups over the years… teachers, students and colleagues.'

Central to Fintan's life, remains God. 'God is key to my life and underpins me, continually recreating us and our world all the time.' But, he will always have time for more marathons, and maybe even improve his golf handicap.

As St Paul's told the people in Greece, everyone can run the good race. Fintan paraphrases it as a mission statement for everyone in life... 'Keep on going right to the end. Keep going to the finish line!'

●●●

John Boyers
RETIRED CHAPLAIN MANCHESTER UNITED FC

JOHN BOYERS WAS brought up in a strong Methodist home in Grimsby. His parents were hard working people. His father, a fish merchant working with his brothers at the local fish docks, hoped that John would take over the family business one day. It was not to be, as John's passion was to become a geography teacher.

John played many sports, with enthusiasm if not skill! As well as football, he enjoyed cricket, tennis and rugby. In college he met his future wife Anne. They got engaged in 1970 and married two years later. John had also begun to discern that God may be calling him to ministry. After getting married, they returned to John's hometown, Grimsby, in the north of England to set up home. They were both teachers and got on with life and linked with John's family Methodist Church.

He still felt the niggle of God's call to train for full-time ministry. He was still attending his local Methodist church, worked with their local youth group and did preaching. In 1975, it became obvious that God was sending him a very clear message. John (and Anne) came to realise that God was calling him to train for Christian ministry.

He went to study theology at London Bible College (now London School of Theology) and got involved in a local baptist church in Watford. Graduation and ordination as a probationary baptist minister took place on the same day in June 1979. He joined the ministry team at St James Road Baptist Church, Watford, where he would eventually become the senior pastor.

John became very involved in his church ministry. He recalls a Saturday morning in 1977 when a visiting minister came to help in training some 'home group' leaders. Mike was a baptist minister and also chaplain at Aldershot FC In conversation, he suggested John should consider volunteering to be chaplain to the local club, Watford, pointing out that staff and players there also had the same pastoral needs as people in his church and its community. A seed was planted.

In the weekly *Watford Observer*, John read the regular column by Graham Taylor, the Watford, and future England, manager. One week it was about, 'The Club and The Community'. Taylor wanted to build strong community links, to bring the club into the community... to make Watford a community club. And he stressed that this was a two-way involvement.

'If you are part of our community and feel you have something to give us, a special skill, an interest or an idea, then I want to hear from you.' That sentence from Graham Taylor struck John. He wrote to Graham about chaplaincy. Taylor arranged a meeting.

'Why should a football club have a chaplain? What would a chaplain do?' Graham asked John. The answer must have been very acceptable.

Initially, the manager said he would try a chaplaincy for a year, but soon John became the official chaplain for the football club, where he provided spiritual and pastoral advice and support to the players and staff during their amazing rise to the top league in England in the period 1977 to '87. After those glorious Taylor years, when Taylor had moved on to Aston Villa and then England, John remained as WFC chaplain until 1992.

'The presence of a club chaplain is of vital importance to some of the people, some of the time. Whether it be a super-star player or part-time cleaner, the challenges and crises of life can hit hard, and periodically life's big questions loom large, too. The regular presence of a trained and trusted chaplain is like a pastoral and spiritual safety net for all.

'In chaplaincy people have to know you. You just can't provide a 'service'. The chaplain is a friend of the people of the club, non-judgemental – whatever is in your life or your personal, social or religious background. We don't impose ourselves, but we are there for everyone.' But John is quick to explain he doesn't have answers to every question. A chaplain is like the local doctor. He's a generalist. Sometimes a doctor's conversation leads to the need for the client to see a specialist. It may be so in chaplaincy. When a chaplain knows he's beyond the limits of his training, it is time for him to seek the client's permission to – confidentially – involve a specialist, maybe a trained counsellor in a specialist field, or a medical specialist, or a sports psychologist.

John has come to understand that anyone in any of the three groups might benefit from chaplaincy – the players, the non-playing staff, and even the fans. But he stresses that he's never wanting to replace a local priest, minister, pastor... or any other faith leader in someone's life.

John's eventual move to Manchester United was not a spontaneous decision, nor something he had dreamed about! During the 1980s he was really enjoying his ministry at Watford. His church commitments were bearing fruit and his voluntary chaplaincy with the club was also bedding down. Other football clubs were noticing the value in having a club chaplain. Because of Watford's rise in football through the divisions, many clubs were looking to Watford to see what they were doing that was special. Several were in touch with John, personally, asking about his role at WFC and advice of appointing their own chaplain.

One of John's calls in 1987 was from Kenneth Merrett, then secretary at Manchester United, who explained that they were considering having a chaplain. This led to an invitation to come up and talk about how football club chaplaincy might work. John went to Manchester to meet informally, but unexpectedly for him, a proposal was presented that he should come on staff to take a similar role at Manchester United, in a full-time, paid capacity. He had been in a part-time volunteer role in Watford.

John's response was, something like... 'It's not about what you are willing to pay me, it is all about what God wants me to do'. He explained that he needed to know what God was directing and guiding him over their suggestion. 'I need to talk with God and listen, and also talk with my wife and listen, too!'

He also explained the crucial importance of a chaplain being engaged in a voluntary capacity. Sports chaplaincy was in its infancy. Development would be hindered if it was modelled as a benefit which would be a cost to the club, for if that were so, smaller, poorer clubs would not appoint chaplains. A voluntary ministry appointed by the club, involving a suitably gifted, trained individual, endorsed by church or denomination, giving a day a week or more to serving the sports club, (but given over to the role by the local church who paid the salary) would work for rich and for poor clubs.

Few clubs could afford a full-time paid chaplain.

Nonetheless, United asked John to consider their offer – and a much better salary than a Baptist minister! He (and his wife) both felt, after prayerful ponderings, that God had not given them a green light to agree to a move to Manchester. He declined their offer graciously, and suggested they might consider a colleague near Manchester, who had a sporting background, and who might be able to volunteer a day per week. This was actually agreed by United.

However, in 1992, Manchester United returned to John with a direct invitation to talk about MU chaplaincy as their chaplain was moving away. In short, they wanted John to become chaplain and they agreed to follow the pattern he had outlined five years earlier. The job was offered to him a second time, as a day and a half per week, as a volunteer to provide chaplaincy services to all employees, staff and players. John, eventually, would arrive and work with Manchester United. But, not before a new organisation called SCORE was formed and properly constituted, which provided support and governance to enable him to develop chaplaincy in sport inter-denominationally in the UK, and sometimes, beyond. It became a charity registered by the UK Charity Commission in 1991.

Soon, John would launch into a full-time role with SCORE. In late summer 1992, he and his family moved up to Manchester and, continuing as National Director of SCORE, would spend a day and a half in chaplaincy at Manchester United. He had discerned God's direction over this second invitation to MU via personal prayer, family, friends and colleagues in and out of sport. 'This was a huge leap of faith for us as a family. Anne was teaching in Watford, and that income was a safety net for us if SCORE failed to find funds to pay my wages. That income stream was lost with the Manchester move. God's grip on us was not lost, though! We said yes to this second invitation because we were sure this was God's purpose and plan being worked out. We knew all would be well.'

Over time, SCORE, grew, continuing to pioneer sports chaplaincy inter-denominationally, and extending its reach from mainly England to other parts of the UK, and to other sports besides football. The Manchester United platform, and support, helped considerably. Potential chaplains were identified, trained, inducted and supported in Rugby Union, Rugby League, County Cricket, and horseracing, and began to emerge in other sports too. Manchester United were hugely understanding of John's role with SCORE and his openness to combine his ministry and his voluntary role with the club.

He began to step back from his 60 hour a week role with SCORE in 2011, when there were about 250 chaplains working mainly with elite sports clubs across the UK He retired in 2018.

SCORE has been renamed Sports Chaplaincy UK, and continues to work across the UK to establish and resource chaplaincy in professional, semi-pro and amateur and local sports clubs. John serves Sports Chaplaincy UK as an International Ambassador, and speaks in local churches and at conferences, but is enjoying being more retired and able to give more time to his wife Anne, their boys Andrew (a sports photographer) and Jonathan (a Baptist minister), their wives and the five grandchildren they have to be spoil!

Through his move to SCORE and national sports chaplaincy development, John moved out of full-time local church ministry, with the relative security it brought. He set out in faith – knowing the presence of God was with him and his wife. He felt clearly that God was leading him to MUFC in 1992, which happened to coincide with the start of the amazingly successful years of Alex Fergusson's management.

'I noticed players making various expressions of faith when coming onto the pitch before a match, but I am not sure how reflective of personal Christian faith it all was,' says John, in reflection. 'For some I'm sure it is authentic, for others maybe not; for some maybe it is just superstition.'

Gradually, people of all Christian denominations, and indeed of all faiths, became very accepting of him at United. In times of worry or anxiety or grief, or when someone needed to talk confidentially, John was the point of contact and call for people in the club. The opening line... 'Hey, Rev... have you got five minutes?' was frequently asked. He has retired as Manchester United's chaplain, and has written a fascinating perspective on life and the world of football in *Beyond the Final Whistle*.

●●●

Philip Mitchell

PASTORAL DIRECTOR FOR SPORTS CHAPLAINCY AND FORMER FOOTBALLER

PHILIP MITCHELL IS from East Belfast. He grew up during the Troubles in the early-70s. His dad worked in the city centre, which was an anxious time for his family as bombs and bomb scares were regular daily life.

At 14 he notes, 'I stuck my flag in the sand!' He committed his life to being a follower of Jesus Christ. He is from a family that went to church, and many families in his area did likewise. It was normal to attend church. As part of his church, he attended the Boys Brigade and Sunday School. Philip was one of the 'messers' in school, but he has fond memories of one Sunday School teacher, David Beasley, who invited all the students to ask a question on anything. He enjoyed these sessions as they opened up the questions on life, questions such as... 'How should you spend Sunday? What is heaven? How will the world end?' He was actively listening to these questions, and, 'This set me off on my journey!'

Philip then embarked on his journey. 'We had bibles in the house, so I started to read and dig into it. I was asking questions... however I never had doubts. I just needed to find my own roots as I had been handed on a faith... I just needed to examine it for myself. I wanted to find out what God expected of me and how did he expect me to act in the world or do things, live my life, find out what was my destiny.'

Reading the bible has remained with Philip as a place of relevance and challenge throughout the rest of his life. He still discovers how this word of God challenges him daily. He loves reading the words of Jesus, the letters of St Paul and even the big stories in the Old Testament where courage emerges. He recalls the words of Joshua (1:9) "I have commanded you to be determined and confident... do not be discouraged or afraid, for I the Lord your God am with you , wherever you go"' For Philip even during his professional football days, the bible was a key source of his faith.

'At 14, I knelt at my bedside and prayed and invited Jesus into my life, and to be with me. For Philip faith was important all through the years of playing football and beyond.

He had a natural talent and ability for football from an early age. Growing up in Belfast he was devoted to the game. He was Leeds United supporter and dreamed from an early age of playing for Northern Ireland.

Growing up in a city with an underlying sectarian tension, Philip just enjoyed playing football with anyone. 'For me, sport helped me understand the different religions. You didn't know what a Catholic looked like, or what he believed. Then you played against them or played with them on the same team, and knew they were a good player. Gradually, I came to realise that I was like him, and he doesn't seem much different to me, he just grew up in a different part of the city!'

But, he remembers being at school and feeling the need to tell people about his newly discovered faith. He began to tell a few close friends, and notes this can be a scary moment for any 14-year-old. He remembers one chat. 'I hear you are a Christian now,' Philip was told, and his friend continued, 'I'd love to be a Christian... I just don't think I could keep all those rules! Well done'.

For Philip, this was significant.

Having the courage to speak about his faith had an unexpected outcome. And he realised on his journey that it wasn't all about keeping rules, and more about talking to God and hearing what God was saying to him through his Word and through people God had placed in his life. As his journey progressed, he realised that obedience brought joy, and disobedience brought despair. And that at the centre of his faith were love and forgiveness, and the need for perseverance and courage.

Philips's dad died when he was 18. For him his dad was a role model, a giant of a man and someone who encouraged him and who was inherently kind. His death was sudden and was a hammer blow to his family. Philip recalls the feeling that he now needed to grow up fast.

Around this age too, he was progressing in football, but he was very conscious that his dad was no longer around. He was encouraged by a few mentors to keep going. He won Irish Schools and Irish Youth winners medals in 1985 with Grosvenor High School and Ards FC.

Philip then broke into senior football in 1987 and played in the Irish League with Ards and Linfield where he won league and Gold Cup medals before moving onto the full-time professional game in England with Ipswich Town. He returned to play in the north at 23, disappointed he hadn't moved to the next level.

'I was an honest professional, not a super talented professional. Yet I worked hard at my game. I was fortunate to play for the two big clubs here, Linfield and Glentoran, and with some great players... and under Roy Coyle.' Philip signed for Portadown on his return to Northern Ireland and played in the European Cup against defending champions Red Star Belgrade , but a year later was on the move again.

Billy Hamilton had begun to put together a team with a lot of experience at Distillery, and Philip would become part of the Distillery teams that won the Gold Cup and went close to winning the league title. He was enjoying his football again.

During all these years, he continued to try to live and express his faith. He speaks about the 'privilege' of being invited to speak about his faith in other churches and to talk openly about what his faith meant. He recalls around 10 other Irish League players who were openly Christian and happy to talk about their faith. He does note that even though he was a practising Christian, 'there were bumps on the road'.

Playing for Glentoran in the last three years of his career was exciting not just from the medal haul of winning league, Gold Cup and most significantly an Irish Cup in 1998, but because he felt most comfortable about himself and his faith. Football was no longer fighting for first place in his life, and he was at his most comfortable to express himself on and off the field

People knew where Philip stood with God and whilst he was never intentionally seeking out conversations, he looks back and hopes that his faith still shone through. There were lots of conversations about faith in the dressing-room that came naturally, and he was joined in the Glentoran dressing-room by a fellow Christian Stuart Elliot, 10 years younger but who significantly went on to play successfully in England and Scotland and for Northern Ireland at international level.

'Stuart was a real talent and together with my experience in years, we encouraged one another on our faith journey and still do to this day.' Philip remembers before games, 'Getting out of the car and praying to God to protect me... give my best, be with me... those prayers become more intentional as I became older'.

Turning 50 was a key milestone for him. It was a time for him to reflect and take stock. He was firm in his belief that he wanted to serve God in whatever plan there was for him, but he didn't have any aspirations. He then talks about how he got involved with Sports Chaplaincy UK and Ireland. His younger brother was approached by Ossie McAuley to work with Sports Chaplaincy for one day a week. 'They suggested that I should do the job, as I had more contacts!' Over the past few years, the role of the voluntary chaplain has increased to more and more clubs. 'Younger people now have less knowledge of faith and the bible. When I played, people knew I was a believer, and the conversation was natural.'

As a former professional footballer Philip is as convinced as ever about his faith. The call to follow Jesus in his life is still strong, and he continues to enjoy talking with people about his faith journey. 'I just want to talk about the "love of God" and allow the work of the cross to speak for itself.' He encourages others to do likewise. He doesn't put labels on people.

'Everybody's journey is different. There is no one path or encounter the same for everyone, but ultimately Jesus is the only answer. There are many issues and challenges for people on their journey but the issue we all have to face is sin. It's an issue of the heart. We have been born into it and only Jesus can provide the answer. I am called to be a witness to Jesus in how I live, and to be salt and light, and to point people to Him. He (Jesus) craves a relationship with us. He died for all of us!'

Philip is now very content with his life balance and making a difference. Being involved in sport is still important to him. He enjoys being able to present complimentary copies of the bible to players… many of whom have never owned a bible, and he is still encountering people whom he meets in sport who have a desire to know Jesus.

Philip would like to be remembered as a 'follower of Christ.'

●●●

Mark Fleming

FOOTBALL CHAPLAIN

MARK FLEMING GREW up an atheist, with no background in church, in the village of Fairlie in the west of Scotland. 'I used to have a few battles with the God squad. It was a total shock to my family when at 17 I became a Christian.'

There was no family faith at home, to such an extent that his dad would not allow his son to join the Boys Brigade. This was due to its connection with a church. The Boys Brigade is an inter-denominational youth organisation with strong Christian roots. 'Faith never featured in my life until my teens,' says Mark. His dad eventually came around to Mark's new found faith..

He remembers how one of his teenage friends 'changed'.

'One day he came in and said he had become a Christian. Up to this he had been a Punk, a Mod… I felt it would be a fad.'

But Mark noticed a change in his friend for the better, however, 'After reading books on various faiths, I concluded that religion was for weak-minded people... religion caused nothing but trouble!'

At the same time, Mark found it difficult to argue against the positive changes he noticed in his friend. Eventually, through his friend's 'witness' Mark gave in and went along to a youth event where people were openly talking about their faith and their story. 'I went away challenged, despite all my best arguments. I concluded that I can't challenge their experience or the evidence that I saw in their lives. There was something different about them. It was real, attractive and spiritual.' This was the beginning of his search for seeking out answers that led him on the path of faith and belief in Jesus.

Initially, he did not take part with an official church or in the words of his dad, a 'bible thumping group!' However, it was not until he got to study computer science at Caledonian University that he could take part in the Christian Union events. This was his first experience of being around any type of Christian community. In the group there were people from many backgrounds, with a common focus on Jesus. He liked the non-denominational tone of the group.

Mark was not really a top sports person, but just happy to play an honest game. He confesses that he has been a lifelong Partick Thistle supporter...'the great Glasgow alternative team!' His grandparents lived nearby, so this was the club he chose to follow.

Mark completely immersed himself in his new-found faith. Through the Christian Union he was discipled by a Malaysian friend. He later attended his church, and developed new friendships there. However, ultimately he did not align too closely with a church. His 'church' was his friends in the Christian Union.

Having come from a completely non-religious background, Mark was curiously now asking all types of questions about faith. He recalls buying his first bible. He describes how he approached reading the bible as, 'Anything I didn't understand, I put a question mark down. Eventually, I was able to get answers to all the questions.' His faith was a questioning faith that led to growth.

Reflecting on this change in his life, he notes, 'Ever since I invited Jesus into my life, I have been on an incredible spiritual journey with God. I have been utterly amazed at how His plan for my life has unfolded... my life could not be in better hands. As a teenager if you had told me that I would become a wholehearted follower of Jesus and a football chaplain, I would have laughed as much as everyone else did when I first told them I had actually become a Christian!'

Mark needed to search for answers to all the questions of faith. Questions such as, 'Who is Jesus?'

'Seek him, you will find him eventually.' He noticed things happening in his life. He became aware of decisions he was making. He was also more aware of his conscience, not immediately, but over a period of time. His journey into faith took time. He does admit that not everyone was convinced, but finally, when he 'got serious with God, folk got serious with me'.

After college Mark became a computer salesman. Eventually, he decided to go to Bible College for a couple of years in Edinburgh. He enjoyed the discipline of this new life, and he began to work with several different churches and denominations. He was helping them do outreach. Eventually, he was asked by one to be the pastor in a Pentecostal-style church.

He was senior pastor at Hopehall Church in Paisley for 10 years, before he moved to Kilsyth Community Church in 1998. This was the same year I started as chaplain to Partick Thistle and before going full time with Sports Chaplaincy Scotland. Sports chaplaincy in Scotland was only emerging at this time in clubs.

A chaplain must accompany people, 'To see past the player and connect with the person'. He sees it as his task to walk alongside people off the pitch and get to know them. 'Chaplains are pastorally proactive,' he states, 'and spiritually reactive.'

Mark's role was a voluntary one, which was attractive for clubs, and his local church helped him manage the dual roles. A gift from faith to sport.

He does not pray for success. 'I strongly advise our chaplains to never take credit for success, so they will not receive the blame for failure. Over the years, when results have not been going Thistle's way, people have often joked with me that it was my fault because I did not pray enough. Believe me, if praying for victory was a legitimate aspect of chaplaincy, Thistle would have won the UEFA Champions League by now! But it doesn't work that way.

'I have always found it a bit of a challenge knowing what to ask for when praying for players. As I have mentioned, we do not pray for divine favour, success, or victory. Christian players are not exempt from injury or disappointment, and I do not believe that God favours them in a sporting context.

'The positive mentoring of young footballers is crucial to their development, and chaplains can play a vital role in this.' Chats with some players can impact on their well-being and performance. Sometimes, his conversations led to prayer moments and spiritual encounters with the players. In his autobiography *Confessions of a Football Chaplain*, he recalls stories of confessions, compromising moments, exorcisms and private moments of acts of faith. However, he never witnessed any prayer in the dressing-room at first hand.

Pastoral support is for the whole club, however, and not just the players. Mark integrated himself into all aspects of the club, from looking after players' families on match day with hospitality, to making weekly visits to the office, to see the staff. 'I was there for everyone, not just the players. That is why I always stress that the chaplaincy role is not primarily a religious one, but more of a pastoral support to people of all faiths and individual beliefs.'

'When I started, I found it difficult just meeting people in church, all believing the same things. In a club, you notice and meet people who are from the world and might think differently to the folk in church. That helped me in my preaching.'

Mark found it easier to meet people where they are at and begin there. He finds that churches have a different starting point at times, and this might not work.

Scottish football has its well-known challenges with sectarianism. Mark was often asked which side he was on, and his well-rehearsed answer was that he was a follower of Jesus! He notes a high energy of banter about his faith. 'Sectarianism remains an issue in Scottish football. Most team do not want to be identified as Protestant or Catholic, so none of our chaplains would identify themselves as either. They simply define themselves as Christian and there is a wide variety of church backgrounds among them.'

Mark advanced to setting up his own mental health business, working with the NHS in Scotland and giving training to clubs. He realised he needed to upskill in this area in order to help people who had some mental health difficulties. He is now part-time as Scottish Director of Sports Chaplaincy UK and part-time delivering mental health training with various sporting bodies.

He still has lingering questions about the institutional church. Nothing about his personal faith has changed. 'Without a doubt, God has been part of my journey in sport. He has opened doors for me. Scottish football is very secular.

To have a huge number of clubs now on board with chaplaincy is amazing. Only God could have done that.'

Mark would like to be remembered for making a positive difference in Scottish sport, as someone who saw the person and not the player, and valued and served people in the same way as God does. 'I've tried to model a different set of values. Hopefully, people will smile as they remember me and say things like, "He meant well!"'

●●●

Martin Lewis

CHAPLAIN AND FORMER RUGBY PLAYER

MARTIN LEWIS WAS a rugby player in the game's pre-professional days, and played and enjoyed rugby, combining it with a job in Lloyds Bank, until he got a serious injury at the age of 42.

Brought up in a Christian home, he was always a believer. He tells the story his mother told people that, as a young boy, he had two dreams either to play rugby for Wales or to be a missionary. 'All these years later doing sports chaplaincy you could say I am a missionary in Wales!'

Around the age of 10 at a camp, he heard something that profoundly challenged him... 'If Jesus came tonight, would you stay or go?!'

'I clearly remember that night, of making a personal commitment to Christ.' At 16 he went to a Luis Palau convention (an Argentine evangelical preacher) in Cardiff. As a result, he made a firmer commitment to his faith. 'A few of my mates were saved... I already had been. I decided it was time to get baptised.' He had felt some pressure to get baptised before, but now understood it was the right moment for him.

'That was a special moment from me, I felt something clearly happen and from then I lived a far more committed Christian life.'

Martin comes from a family of a Brethren background. His dad was someone, he fondly remembers, who would go anywhere to talk about the Gospel. Martin no longer attends the Brethren Church but attends a large church in Cardiff.

At 6'8", he was always picked for the basketball or rugby teams. Though, rugby was his passion and his dream as a young man. 'I played at every level and just missed out on playing International rugby.' He had 12 years of first-class rugby, playing over 400 games in front of large crowds for Penarth, Bridgend and Abertillery. His career ended when a snapped ACL at the age of 42.

From the age of 19 he began work, and had to combine the balance of a job and sport, but he continued to be involved in his faith. This was crucial for him. 'At an amateur level you gave it your all... you had to train hard, but you still had to go to work regardless of the result or whatever else was happening.' At this time he was also a youth leader in his local church and in his early-twenties became a house deacon, and led local house groups and prayer groups.

'I have always been able to combine my two passions. Early on I decided not to play rugby on a Sunday. This might seem big now, but back then there were very few games on a Sunday.'

Rugby, around this time, was a Saturday and weekday sport. He recalls playing for Bridgend when he was the only non-international in the team and on one occasion having to confront his coach, telling him, 'I'm sorry, it's Sunday... I'm not playing'. He was informed, 'If you don't train, you won't be in line for selection'. Martin was benched.' Then, before the next game on a Saturday, the team was read out. He was on the list. 'I saw that as amazing, as God honours those who honour him. I do get playing on a Sunday, but it's a personal decision for everyone.'

Martin is often asked by young parents about the challenge of balancing a Sunday with young children who want to play sport and are part of a family that attends church. 'It is all about balance. Don't say no totally to sport, but try to make sure it's not sport only... get a balance.' When he is dealing with professional sports players, he suggests they try to attend church before a match. He tries to challenge them to connect to the 'Body of Christ' even if they cannot be a regular church-goer.

Martin has spoken with senior people in the Welsh rugby union and has pointed out that in a more cosmopolitan world, that space is allowed for people who have and express their values and beliefs. 'This has to be accommodated. It's about well-being and looking after the individual.' Martin believes too that a team culture should accommodate individuals who have different values.

'You want that individual to feel the best and go out and do their best.'

Martin is chaplain at Cardiff Blues and he notes some of the overseas players, like the South Africans, Maoris or Pacific Islanders, are generally much more open to having faith support. 'If a Welsh lad says he has faith, he gets some jokey comments.'

Out of the blue, he was asked if he'd like to replace Ian Rees as the Cardiff Blues' chaplain, a challenge he accepted after praying about it.

He began to work with the underage teams and gradually worked his way up to the academy, and later the first team. 'God kept opening the doors in different ways.'

Martin remains a volunteer chaplain. 'What we offer is that non-judgemental, impartial listening ear... totally confidential, unless of course there are safeguarding issues. We've got this tagline, "Pastorally proactive, spiritually reactive". We're not there to bible-bash, but to try to be the hands and feet of Jesus.'

He recently passed 10 years in the role. There are now almost 100 chaplains in Wales across many different sports, with 55 working in rugby union. Sports Chaplaincy UK, of which Martin is a member, has 600 chaplains at work.

Martin is full of gratitude for his life, and the opportunities he has met. His great hope is that God is placing chaplains in clubs for a reason, to offer hope. 'Being a person of Christ in a club is important.' He recognises that not everyone in a club can relate to a church, but hopes that they might just relate to the local club chaplain. He is also involved in community work, with Blues' players helping to feed homeless people in Cardiff at his behest.

'What I like about chaplaincy is that you are just being with people at crucial and ordinary moments in their life.'

Sportspeople can learn from having others come in from outside and who see life in a different way. That's the value of what a chaplain can bring to a club. 'We come with a slightly different skill-set and view of the world into that insular bubble, so we see things that others don't always spot.'

Martin's only real regret from his playing days is, 'Not being as vocal about my faith, even though I took a stance'. He also regrets not being able to play rugby now!

'It is a form of loss. If you love sport... you love sport!' For him, he would like to be remembered with the words... 'To God be the Glory!'

●●●